DIALOGUES ACROSS THE DIVIDE

Conversations with Spirits

Compiled and transcribed by
JUSTINE REDDEN

from audio recordings of trance sessions with:

Teacher - Angela Ramcke.
Paul Phillips (AKA The Boy)
Chris Jones
Justine Redden
Theresa Edwards
Tracey Cannon
Beth Rees
Gemma Whitbread
Peter Jones (AKA Our Pete)
Jill Davies

Copyright © Justine Redden

Edited by Alana Davies

First published in paperback September 2024

Justine Redden has asserted her right under the Copyright, Designs & Patents Act 1988, to be identified as the author of this work.

The writings in this book are not the opinions of the group or its individual members. It is the transcript of the audio recordings of the trance sessions.

All rights reserved. No part of this publication may be reproduced, stored in a retrieval system, or transmitted, in any form or by any means without the prior written permission of the publisher, nor be otherwise circulated in any form of binding or cover other than in which it is published and without a similar condition being imposed on the subsequent purchaser.

Published by © AC Publishing

Cover image by
Ian David Spencer - Visionary Artist
www.iandavidspencer-artist.co.uk

Grateful thanks are extended to our sponsor,
Danny Edwards, of Aries Stairlifts
www.ariesstairliftsltd.co.uk
Tel: 01792 844765 / 07773 352914
Email: info@ariesstairlifts.co.uk

CONTENTS   PAGE

INTRODUCTION   9

SESSION

#	Date		Year	Page
1	24th	November	2021	20
2	-	December		23
3	16th	March		31
4	30th	March		35
5	28th	April		39
6	11th	May		46
7	25th	May		56
8	22nd	June		64
9	6th	July	2022	72
10	13th	July		70
11	3rd	August		86
12	24th	August		95
13	21st	September		101
14	5th	October		105
15	9th	November		118
16	30th	November		125
17	4th	January		132
18	22nd	February		140
19	15th	March	2023	148
20	29th	March		156
21	17th	May		166

	SESSION			PAGE
22	24th	May		177
23	21st	June		184
24	19th	July		192
25	23rd	August		201
26	6th	September		210
27	4th	October		215
28	25th	October		220
29	15th	November		232
30	Xmas	December		242
31	31st	January		252
32	7th	February		262
33	14th	February		271
34	22nd	February	2024	283
35	6th	March		293
36	13th	March		306
37	Golden Ticket Night			324

THIS GRAVEYARD
A Poem by Justine Redden

This graveyard's cold to the touch; tombstones sit like guardians of the empty bodies which lie below, inscribed with earth names and birth and death dates and messages from the heart. Ascending souls recognise these earthly writings as regards to themselves and smile in fond remembrance of the life just passed.

This graveyard's solitary tree throws open its arms in a joyous welcoming embrace, and nods its full green head in glad recognition of the continuance of the soul. This graveyard is not a cold place, not a place of doom and gloom. The quiet hush is not an eerie silence, but a warm and peaceful contemplation.

This graveyard is a meeting place for the souls of the departed; it is a place of homecoming, a joyful reunion with the ones we thought had gone forever. This graveyard is not a place of darkness and despair; it is a place of light and laughter in meeting loved ones there.

This graveyard is never still. The air hums and vibrates in tune with the Divine source, and shimmers in pinks and blues and golden hues, as souls say goodbye one last time, to the bodies of this incarnation. This graveyard, like any other, is a place of light and love, beauty and colour, laughter and hope.

Introduction

We are a small group of like-minded individuals who are able to communicate with the spiritual realms. We are all at different stages of our spiritual development and mediumship and we all have different strengths and abilities. We have been brought together (by spirit) to share this wonderful journey of discovery, enlightenment and spiritual wisdom and to share that knowledge and those experiences with the world.

There are many different ways in which mediums can work to be able to give accurate evidence of the existence of the afterlife. We are greatly privileged to be able to perform transfiguration. This is mediumship on a physical level. The medium sits in a large custom-made booth and a red light is shone on him/her. This enables the harnessing of the energy and it allows the spirit communicators to blend their energies with the medium's. This results in amazing visual and vocal demonstrations of proof that life still goes on after the demise of the physical body. The method the spirit-being uses is to overshadow the features onto the face, neck, hands and sometimes the whole body of the sitting medium. The spirit-being is able to manipulate the medium's voice-box and speak in their own language and accents.

A female spirit can overshadow a male medium and use his voice-box and vice-versa. This often results in very amusing visuals and vocals, even singing. We have several main spirit communicators who join us every time we sit in trance, and many other communicators who have been waiting for an opportunity to briefly 'come back' into a physical body for the purpose of showing themselves to us and sharing information and their stories with us.

Sometimes these conversations are hilarious as those spirit-beings are exactly the same characters in the spirit world as they were when they were on the earth-plane. To capture the true personalities of the spirit communicators, their stories, jokes or complaints, the (bad) language they use and their style of speaking is documented exactly as they say it.

Some of the names have been spelled phonetically as some communicators have been in the spirit world for many years, even centuries in some cases, and were unable to read or write when they were on the earth-plane. This book is a combination of these conversations, questions and answers and the wisdom and knowledge shared with us from our dear friends in the spirit world. As it is in chronological order it is also an ongoing record of our own individual spiritual development, knowledge and experiences and insights into our personal lives and events. By **'Spreading the Word'** of the existence of the afterlife and the overwhelming and all-encompassing, unconditional love of spirit, it is our heart-felt hope that we can spread positivity and joy and help people gain an understanding of life – past, present and future.

Our main trance mediums are **Paul (AKA The Boy)** and **Chris.** They are exceptional trance mediums with exceptional abilities and they never fail to be successful channels for the spirit world communicators. Without their dedication to spirit, these trance sessions would not happen and this book could not have been written. Justine is a developing trance medium and hopes to become as amazing as the boys in time. We have all dipped our toes in and had a go sitting in the box! But it is not for everyone, as already mentioned we are all mediums and have our own strengths and abilities in other aspects of mediumship.

Our teacher is Angela, she is a very talented and experienced medium, teacher and healer. She has guided, supported, coaxed and cajoled us to develop our abilities to the absolute best possible. One of her favourite sayings is 'Don't put the phone down yet!' By saying this she pushes us to ask for more information and more evidence from the spirit communicators. She is an inspiration and we are very grateful for everything she does for us. She also is responsible for protecting the sitting trance mediums from this side of life. She is very highly respected by our friends in the spirit world who are extremely grateful for everything she does. Again, without her dedication, protection and belief in us, this book could not have been written.

Several of our mediums in the group are also amazing healers. The other mediums are Jill, Peter (AKA Our Pete), Theresa, Tracey, Beth, Gemma and Rob, Mark and Peter R (PR). Some other names are mentioned as we have had the occasional visitor to the trance sessions.

Although the popular term for developing mediums is a 'circle' of mediums, for the purpose of this book we are known as a group. We are all completely committed to the continuous development of our abilities, in order to provide evidence of the existence of the spirit world and the survival and ongoing journey of all human souls, and the progression of the human spirit as creations of God. We work in Light and Love with the greatest intentions to Spread The Word and to Help and Heal.

Our regular spirit communicators are:
Albert – he channels through Paul (The Boy) and is his main communicator. He is known as the caretaker/facilitator of the trance sessions from spirit side. He organises and guides the spirit communicators who are waiting to come through, and alongside our guides and helpers he protects us. Each communicator has to go past him before communicating with us. The use of bad language is frowned upon in the spirit world and those who do swear are told off in no uncertain terms by Albert. He keeps a Shepherd's Crook by his side to hook around the necks of the unfortunate communicator who oversteps the mark, and they are swiftly pulled away!

Albert was an Oxford University professor in his last life on the earth-plane and he continues to teach in his classroom in the spirit world. The subjects he teaches are vastly different from what is taught on earth. This is expanded on further on in the book.

Colin Jones from Porth in the Welsh valleys – he is a regular communicator whom Albert tolerates! He does tend to be a bit naughty and swears a lot. However, he comes through when the energies (vibrations) are dipping for whatever reason. He makes us laugh and this brings the energy back up. Spirits need lots of energy to be generated to facilitate them to come through. He channels through Paul.

Cornelius Chambers – he was an investigative journalist for The Times newspaper in London in his last earth-life. He likes to say it as it is. Nothing that happens on the earth-plane goes unnoticed in the spirit world, and he always has plenty to say. He teases Chris mercilessly as he finds him very attractive. His teasing is always hilarious but never offensive. He is a very good friend of Albert. He channels through Paul.

Gethin – he is a very well-spoken gentleman who channels through Chris. His input into our spiritual development is to introduce experiments to sharpen our clairvoyance abilities and also to bring through communicators. He worked with us for many months but is currently undergoing teachings himself on the Higher Levels. This is a huge privilege for him. Hopefully, at some time he will return to continue his valuable input into our group.

Matthew – he is another soul that likes to speak his mind. He sometimes says things that Albert would have preferred him not to. He can be a bit thoughtless with regards to how what he is saying is being received by us, but he means well. He has had a block put on his voice for this reason and so it is often very difficult to hear what he is saying. He likes to swear at times too, much to Albert's disapproval. He channels through Chris and is currently his main communicator. Matthew loves to smoke his pipe!

Chow Ling – he is a very old Chinese monk. He is an ancient healing guide and works with the healers in this group. He also gives us physical, mental and emotional healing when it is needed. He always knows when it is needed without being asked. He channels through Paul.

White Eagle – he is a North American Indian who often begins the communications through Paul with chanting and bestowing of prayers and a blessing upon us all. He is a very powerful spirit. He calls us 'MARANBAY' which means 'HIS PEOPLE'.

As a group we have group guides and helpers, but we all also have our own individual guides and helpers. These lovely souls will be introduced throughout the text, along with the spirit communicators. We are greatly honoured and privileged to have been assigned a member of *The Legion* to each of us. ***The Legion* are a group of highly advanced souls from the Higher Levels. They are known as** *Ambassadors of The Legion.* They also work with us and surround us in cloaks of protection.

In this book, the trance mediums are identified in **<u>bold letters and underlined</u>** at the beginning of their time in the box. The spirit communicators are identified in bold *italics* and their messages are in italics.
  Some subjects that we have discussed with the spirit communicators may be deemed controversial. For this

reason those discussions are not documented. Some of the spirit communicators would be identifiable if their real names were used, and as they may have surviving family members, their names have been changed in order to protect their identities and in compliance with the Confidentiality Act 2010. Some subjects are discussed a couple of times but with different communicators.

Although we have been holding trance sessions for a few years, it was only at the end of 2021 that we decided to begin to document the information given to us via these wonderful interactions and communications. We started taking notes and then, with spirit's permission, we began to record them to catch every word and emotion.

Some other terms used:
The Queue - this is comprised of thousands of spirit-beings awaiting their opportunity to come through to us. The Boy sees this when he is in trance. It is as far and as wide as the eye can see. Sometimes The Boy will go into a huge auditorium where there are thousands of spirit-beings watching our trance sessions on a huge screen. They love to

watch and listen to us and love to hear us laughing, it makes them laugh too.

Tasks/teachings/learning opportunities - We all have to achieve objectives that are planned by ourselves in conjunction with our spirit guides and helpers, before we reincarnate back to the earth-plane. Learnings and task completions continue in the spirit world too. Eg, spirit-beings have to learn how to communicate with human beings such as mediums.

The Golden Ticket night - We planned this event in which we all invited a friend or family member to witness a trance session. It took a long time to happen because of personal issues in the lives of our mediums, but we got there eventually. It is the last session in this book.

The most important thing of all is to spread the word of The Almighty, which is Love. It is hoped that this book will help share the wonderful knowledge of the continuous presence and great love of The Almighty, the existence of the spirit world (the after-life) and the continuance and progression of the human soul. We never die, we just transition. Hopefully this shared knowledge will help transform lives and make this world a much nicer, kinder place to live in for all life on this beautiful planet.

SESSION 1
24.11.21

Chris

Gethin – He welcomes us saying *'It's going to be a special night tonight, there will be an opportunity for a visual demonstration of Albert. There are 3 individuals in spirit with us at the moment, they will show themselves, 2 female, 1 male.'*

Working with all of our guides is a true celebration of unity between our two worlds, bringing both together as ONE. I, WE, US, all in participation.

Paul AKA THE BOY.

White Eagle – opening with a chant and prayer to give us protection and a blessing. He tells us that his people are standing behind him, along with his son **Red Eagle**. He *says, 'My people are very peaceful but are often misunderstood. MARAMBAY means MY PEOPLE.'*

Albert - He *says, 'There is powerful energy here tonight. Spirits volunteer and are invited to communicate with you.'*

Someone asks him about managing stress in this world. He replies, *'Imagine your life as a pint of water being held with your arms outstretched – how long does it take to become uncomfortable to hold? STRESS is the water, it makes it painful. The longer you hold it, the more painful it becomes – EMPTY THE WATER!'* Albert advises us to speak from the heart and from our life experiences when we are speaking to the public, during demonstrations of mediumship. He says that we will give more to the audience using **Heart Knowledge.**

A new *Oriental spirit* comes through. His name is **CHI CHI LONG.** He has come through for Our Pete. He *says, 'You are a master healer, you must give healing.'* Our Pete acknowledges this and thanks him for the advice.

Chow Ling – He was 130 years old when he passed back to the spirit world in 837AD. He is a very wise man. He is Mark's Mongolian guide but he is also our group guide and healing guide who works with us when we give healing to others. He had been a warrior before he became a monk. When he was on the earth-plane he lived on a mountain top, only drank water and walked great distances every day. He has a very curved spine, white hair and a large forehead. His voice is very soft and gentle. He has no desire to reincarnate as he sees our world and our lives as a battlefield. He advises us all to live a simple life as far as possible, but to the full. He tells us that our lives are mapped out and when our time is up it is up. No accidents – all is planned. He kindly reassures Mark that he will be with him to help him on his journey. He says to Ange, *'Your pain will be helped by the breakthrough of new pain discoveries. This has been developed in the spirit realms and can perform top to toe scans and will treat the problems at the same time.'* Before he leaves he tells us that he is also ***Albert's*** teacher and promises to come through again. He reminds us that we can call on him at any time for mental, physical and emotional healing and he will come.

A beautiful ***Japanese lady*** comes through, she is singing and gracefully moving her arms in her robes. She is Ange's guide. She puts her hand to her heart and sends love to Ange. Ange thanks her and is quite emotional. The session runs out of time.

SESSION 2
December 2021..

Chris

Gethin comes through joking that he is Chris's warm up act. He says that it is a pleasure and an honour to bring the two worlds together and we all say the same to him. We decided in the last trance session (with Albert's agreement), to hold a question and answer session with us asking the questions and our spirit communicators providing the answers. **Gethin** tells us there are 3 other spirits with him and they will all endeavour to answer all of our questions.

    Gethin *explains, 'Much of the spirit world works through the power of love. The feelings between the spirit world and the earth-plane increase the love, without the physical shell* (the body, sometimes referred to 'the uniform' or 'shell') *all feelings are greatly increased. Remove the shell and the feelings will flow much better. You will be blown away by the intensity of love – it is too wonderful to behold as a human being.'*

    He advises us that writing, thought and prayer are extremely effective forms of communication, and that the focus and energy we use to see the auric colours, the overshadowing and the changes on the medium is essential.

Q1. How did we come together as a group? Was it on purpose?
A. *'Yes, but you made the free choice to participate as you have free will. A little nudge in the right direction was all that was needed from us. Remember, everything is thought – guides receive these thoughts and get the ball rolling from spirit-side. As it is spirit's intention to communicate with you, the thoughts then become one. Guides on Higher Levels guide those in spirit, your guides and helpers guide you here – it is done by thought and colour. This is a golden opportunity for you all.'* A tear of love rolls down Chris's face to demonstrate the great strength of love.

Q2. What can we do to become more spiritual and to enhance our spiritual development?
A. *'The earth-plane is occupied by plant, animal and human shells. Each human is at a different level of spirituality, you are here for your own experiences and learning. If you wish to elevate and promote peace on earth you are on a higher*

level than those who don't. ALL of us have been here hundreds of times before. When you reincarnate back to the earth-plane it will be to a higher level. Meditation is strongly advised, reading some of the books on spiritual development and human experiences is also a very good way to gain knowledge but remember to be mindful of what you are reading.'

Q3. Paul asks about his spiritual pathway.

A. **Gethin** says, *'Thank you Paul for what you are doing in trance, allowing spirit to work with and through you.'* He goes on to say that Paul is always going to work with spirit. He has been told in his sleep-state what outlines his path ahead and it is a very successful pathway. He will work less in his normal day to day employment and his spiritual work will increase in the very near future.

Before he leaves, **Gethin** says, *'There is significant desire to work with each one of you and an endless wealth of commitment and loyalty to you all from spirit. You are continuing to show great commitment to spirit and will be rewarded. You are on a wonderful path and opportunities will present themselves.'* He reminds us that our guides and loved ones hear us, our thoughts are received and acted upon without impacting on our free choice.

Paul AKA The Boy.

Albert welcomes us, he *says, 'Dear friends, welcome to this correspondence evening. We will endeavour to answer all of your questions. There are over 13,000 (spirit) people in the hall behind me, it looks like a school photo! They are all watching this happening on what can only be described as a big screen. They are waiting patiently for their opportunity to work with you.'* We wave to them by waving at the box and we say hello. Albert stated that he felt a wave of energy rip right through him when we waved.

Q4. 'I don't feel like you are working with me anymore. Why is that?'

A. ***Albert*** replies, *'Your mind is elsewhere, you must focus and ask your guides for help, that is what they are waiting for. If you don't ask for help, they can't give it to you. Guides will guide. Of course you are also welcome to send your thoughts to myself and Gethin but don't forget about your* *guides. They know you far better and have been with you for many, many years.'*

Q. 'When you die, do you go to heaven, hell or purgatory?'
A. **Albert** *replies, 'We ALL go to heaven. There are different levels. There is a darkness in both worlds but there is a path set out for all of us. If you need to seek forgiveness, do so and move on.'* He reassures us by saying *'You are all safe and protected.*

Q6. 'If someone takes their own life, is it frowned upon?'
A. *'Takings one's own life is not frowned upon but it is usually a repeat of a past life. They have usually taken their own life in other incarnations and they are known as repeat offenders. There is always a path to follow but that soul is ill because they cannot accept healing. Their guides will try their hardest to prevent the suicide but they are not always successful. As a result, life fulfilment has not been reached and tasks have not been completed, therefore they have to return to the earth-plane again quite quickly.'*

Q7. 'What is the reason for my relative's mental health problems?'

A. *'It is part of their life-plan. They will have tasks to complete associated with poor mental health in order to learn from that experience. When they pass over all ailments will be gone. Be assured that there are no ill people in the spirit world.'*

Q8. 'Why do some healers have stronger healing abilities than others?'

A. *'All healers have healing guides, their presence is equal. However some healers lack concentration and do not switch off from distractions. This will affect their healing ability as it will dilute the effect. Dedication and trust in our guides and helpers are at the forefront of all healers. Mother Earth herself also needs to be healed.'*

Q9. 'When a person has committed a crime do they go to hell?'

A. *'There is NO punishment – there is education. They must see the error of their ways and seek forgiveness. There are negative forces that try to creep in but our guides protect us so they cannot. Keep saying your prayers before bed. The power of prayer is immense.'*

Q10. 'Why is it easier for healers to see and hear spirit when giving healing than at other times?'
A. *'You need to blend the two. Confidence in healing is as necessary as confidence in other forms of mediumship. A healer works on a higher level. He jokes to Tracey, 'Stop snoring in meditation1!'*

Q11. 'Do we need to ask for specific guides?'
A. *'ALL guides will step forward when asked for help. We stay with our loved ones for eternity, we all knew each other before in past lives. Guides differ, but there are always two or three guides constantly at your side and others will join in as needed. The guide who knows the answer to the question will step up.'*

Q12. 'Do we have the same desires in spirit as we did on the earth-plane?'
A. *'No, there is no need for material things or greed as there is on the earth-plane. There is nothing wrong with making*

an honest living on the earth-plane and there is nothing wrong with having a lovely home and lovely possessions, but there are people who will trample over everyone else to get what they want.'

These are just a few questions we asked at this time. More questions are asked in each trance session and responses documented.

Albert **reminds us to 'Always remain positive, keep away from darkness and negativity. Don't believe everything you see and hear, teach this to your children – encourage them to keep an open mind. Concentrate on the NOW. Put all of your energy into positive thoughts and actions. SPREAD THE WORD.'**

SESSION 3
16.03.22

Paul AKA The Boy

The first communicator to come through is ***Myingbay***. He is Tracey's Aborigine healing guide. He scolds her, saying *'You are not participating in the medicine.'* He promises that he will sit with her and is encouraging her to bring complementary and alternative therapies into her healing. He advises, *'Concentrate on roots and leaves. There is so much more you can do to help. Everything is in nature. Start with a tonic.'* Tracey promises that she will look into these methods of healing. ***Myingbay*** also tells Our Pete that healing is his path and advises him to concentrate on 'mental' healing.

Albert – The group had been discussing the general state of the world and current affairs before the trance session started. Albert had been listening to our comments. He advises *'DEVELOP - DO NOT DISCUSS POLITICS – STOP GOSSIPING.'* He tells Ange that as the disciplinarian she must bring it under control. He says, *'Talking about controversial subjects only brings the energy down. MEDITATE, COMMUNICATE, WHEN YOU DO YOU WILL BE GUIDED.'* He encourages us to practice meditation more as practice makes perfect, and to make our homes a sanctuary, listen to music, light a candle, do what makes us feel happy and relaxed before we start to meditate.

Patrick - He is a fishmonger from London who used to work in Billingsgate fish market. He has come through in previous trance sessions and he has a lot to say for himself. Unfortunately, those sessions were not recorded or documented. He is our next communicator. He says to Ange, *'How's it going Blondie? Get your questions in, I'll answer them and then bugger off!'* **Albert** tells him off for swearing. He tells us that he likes coming to say hello. He says he was married twice and both his wives are in the spirit world with him. He was asked if that presented any problems. He replies, *'No, but they both nag me now! Everyone in the spirit world gets on, there is no malice or jealousy.'* We talk with him for a while but then he leaves to allow other communicators through. He says, *'See you soon, happy days!'*

Solomon – He has not been through before. He was aware of our group and had asked to come. He tells us that we (group) have a fan club in spirit! There are very few groups in the country that perform trance mediumship and we are quite in demand. There are thousands of spirits who want to come through, they are all waiting in a vast queue. He tells us that when he passed into the spirit world, he was told that he would have an opportunity to come through to this group. He says, *'It's an absolute privilege to meet you all.'* He has to go then but promises to come through again.

***Albert* returns then** – Tracey asks him how many levels of spirit are above him? He replies that there are 11 levels above him. He says, **'THE SHINING ONES ARE ON THE TOP LEVEL.'** He wants to stay where he is for now as he wants to continue to meet up and work with us. He says that he will bring some of his elders through soon. He reminds us that we need to learn, listen, feel and trust ourselves. They (spirit) want to work with us for a long time. He says, **'This place** (the community centre we are in) **is our sanctuary. Leave personal issues and politics at the door. You will all have wonderful spiritual experiences, do not take it for granted.**

Don't be afraid. Remember the message – discipline within the group, joviality is welcome – politics is not. LIKE ATTRACTS LIKE – WE WANT ENERGY, HEALING AND LOVE.'

SESSION 4
30.03.22

Chris

Several spirits come through but only for short periods of time. They were just showing themselves via the overshadowing.

Paul

A Native American Indian comes through, he is **Chief Red Moon,** *White Eagle's grandfather.* He is the chief of the **Chuckenowra** Tribe. He says that he feels very privileged to meet us but is troubled by our world as it is now. He says, *'Your world is not as I know it.'* Ange asks why we choose to reincarnate back to this world as it is. He replies, *'Reincarnation is a path written for you. The purpose is to educate you and others – LIFE IS A TEST.'* Someone asks, 'How are guides chosen?' *Red Moon* answers **'THE ALMIGHTY** *chooses. You will find your guides are like for like, they match you. There has to be a balance.'* He is then asked how long he has been in spirit. He replies, *'There is no* *time in the spirit world. On earth Mother Nature shows the time. We have all had many lives.'*

Colin comes through briefly and tells us that his motorbike isn't working as there isn't any petrol over there! He has also hurt his back doing the garden and he is complaining that it is taking all of his time. Of course, there is no illness, disability or pain in the spirit world and spirit can fix everything themselves anyway. He moans that he still hasn't got any teeth yet either!

Albert comes through – he tells us that he is going to bring someone very special through. This spirit-being is very tall. He has black hair, dark eyes and dark eyebrows. He is wearing a gown with oriental type sleeves and is sitting with his arms folded into them. He *says, 'My name is Gabriel. I am from Greece and I am a philosopher. I am privileged to meet you all.'* He tells us that when he was last on the earth-plane he was a teacher and Ange was one of his students. He says that he and Ange used to sit on a rock and talk about the existence of the spirit world. He says, *'She completed her scholarship but was taken as a bride by the Roman soldiers.*

She was 20 years old at that time and she was never seen by her family again. The Roman soldiers took her because she was full of drive and determination and they also took other young girls.'

He tells us that he loved Egypt as he had lived and taught there too. He is very appreciative to have been given the opportunity to come through. He has been in spirit for a long time and has no desire to reincarnate. He tells us that he is at the stage in his development where he neither wants to come back nor would be allowed to. He wants to give us these words of wisdom: ***'FILL YOUR HEARTS WITH JOY, LAUGHTER AND POSITIVITY. ALL OF YOUR GUIDES WILL COME THROUGH IN MEDITATION AND TRANCE. MEDITATION IS THE KEY. COMMUNICATION BETWEEN COLLEAGUES IS PARAMOUNT – IT'S ABOUT LEARNING, DO NOT LOOK BACK.'***

Albert returns – He *says, 'Keep up the good work, this group CANNOT be broken. It is nice to see Peter R again, he has been welcomed. I have to love you and leave you now, our time together this evening has run out.'* Albert would like to have much longer trance sessions but unfortunately we are limited by the closing time of the community centre we are in.

When Paul returns he tells us that there were thousands of people watching us on the big screen. They love humour and really laugh at us when we are laughing.

SESSION 5
28.04.22

Justine

A male spirit is coming through, strong overshadowing, he has a plump face with a grey moustache, a pointy nose, and his skin is dark. He is showing that he had suffered a stroke which had left him with a left sided weakness.

A female spirit is coming through, her eyes are open. Someone asks if her name is Rose and she confirms this by smiling and nodding.

Another male spirit coming through. Tracey believes that this is her brother Andrew. He has thinning hair, a goatee and moustache, and he looks very sad. Justine is still not talking and she is finding this frustrating.

Paul

A strong, powerful male spirit is coming through. He appears to be Native American, chanting and bestowing prayers and blessings on us all. He says, *'We are all part of the same soul family. The world is very different from how it used to be. It is not what anyone wants but there is little anyone of us can do – it is written. It's a learning curve. When you return to the spirit world, you will teach your learnings from this life to others. We also teach here in the spirit world. It is part of our role in this life. There are negative souls on the earth plane who misuse their positions of power and are greedy. There has always been greed but for them what they already have is never enough.'*

We all agree that we are seeing this greed, misuse of power and inequality on a daily basis in varying degrees, and we feel upset that the world is in the state that it is in because of the actions of the greedy.

Albert. He tells us that although this trance session hadn't been planned by Ange, he had known it was going to take place. Chris asks him if anyone else is going to develop in trance mediumship and he replies that we will find out soon enough. He tells us to ask Paul about the 'little nudge' he had given him earlier today when Paul was out shopping for a suit. He had guided Paul to try on a tweed jacket just like one that he *(Albert)* would have worn when he was a professor in Oxford University in his last earth life. **Albert** had found this highly amusing and later on when we asked Paul about this, he confirmed that that had happened exactly as Albert had described. He had been very tempted to buy the jacket but it had been too small. He says it wasn't his normal style either.

Albert tells us that there are big changes coming in the future but we will all still be able to attend our group meetings. This hints at some type of restrictions being placed on our liberties but we will just have to wait and see what happens. He goes on to *say 'Things are being amplified by the media, remember, you can't believe everything you see, hear or read, you have to use your gut instinct. Shut out the media, then your mental health will improve. Money, power and greed are the root of all of the problems in the world.'* He leaves then to bring the first communicator through.

Shirokiya. He is a Japanese spirit, this is the first time that he has come through. He tells us that he had died in the Chow war (there was a dispute between China and Japan with respect to the sovereignty of the Loo Chow Islands, so his death may be in reference to this). He tells us, *'The land was very scarce and there were many fights over it. My father* *also died in that battle. The emperors were greedy, they wanted everything to themselves.'* He had been a farmer and advises us to grow our own food. Beth asks if the legend of the Mashita Gold in the Philippines is true. He confirmed that it is true. He says that he is happy to have had the chance to come through and then says goodbye.

Colin. He says to PR, *'Not you again, you're like part of the bloody furniture!'* He gets told off for swearing by Albert who is standing close by with the Shepherd's Crook! **Colin** tells us that he has finished working on his bike and has been gardening but has hurt his back. (He hasn't really hurt his back as this cannot happen but he likes to get sympathy from us!) When asked why he does these hobbies, **Colin** replies, *'We still have needs – you know what I mean!'* He tells PR how lucky he is to be married to Ange! He jokes that he'd give 'half a crown' for her! **Colin** really enjoys coming through to speak to us, he's allowed to as he lifts the vibrations if they have dipped for some reason. We always love to hear his jokes and he always makes us laugh. He says, *'One day I'm going to come through Chris, that'll shock him!'*

Chow Ling – he tells us that we need reassurances as what is going on in the world currently is alarming and distressing. We will receive healing and answers. He tells Ange that she must seek alternative natural forms of pain relief, for example Haldi (Turmeric*). 'Buy it raw – make paste with boiled water then drink. 1 teaspoon every morning with lemon. It will relieve the inflammation, ginger is a miracle root.'* Chow Ling gives us all healing by sending it through our joined hands. Then, as if he has absorbed all the negative energy, he coughs as if getting rid of the bad pain and illness (like in the film The Green Mile.)

Solomon. He says that he has only come for a short time to help build the energies. He is not a man of many words. Rob asks if a recording of the trance sessions would be allowed. **Solomon and Albert** agree to this.

PR stated that he had a very intense experience and dreamt that he was a French farmer in a past life. **Solomon** told him that it was true.

Tracey asks, 'When we meditate, where does the experience come from - is it a past life?' She had felt euphoria in her dream-state recently. Solomon says, *'The state of euphoria is a wonderful gift, when energies blend together a state of euphoria exists.'* He then says to us all, *'Stay outside, meditate, clear your mind.'* He goes on to say that the Spirit world is working to build our confidence. *'Only a fraction of the human brain is being used – we are sponges, we must be dedicated and meditate. There is no harm to come here. Don't let negativity in.'*

Albert returns. He tells us that we have to live our lives to the full. **'when we empty our minds the Spirit world downloads knowledge into it. Through stillness comes inspiration.'** He tells us that the Spirit world is teaching both sides of soldiers in the Ukraine war. *'**Wars are pointless,** for the soldiers it is a job, it's not up for debate. The development of human kind is tenfold.'*

Before he leaves he says to us all, *'Thoughts are the most powerful energy. **THOUGHTS FROM THE SPIRIT WORLD TO US ARE POSITIVE ENLIGHTENMENT. Don't let negativity come into your thoughts,** keep thoughts to the Spirit world different from your everyday thoughts.'* He promises that he will give us more spiritual guidance and tells us that we will be a collective group for years to come.

They will work with Justine to develop her trance mediumship ability but at a slower pace so as not to scare her. He tells Theresa that she must ask her guides to come to her in a dream state.

SESSION 6
11.05.22

Justine

A female spirit coming through, she appears about 60-70 years old. Her skin appears fluorescent, there is prominent facial twitching, and she is smiling. She has dark hair on top of her head, and she is wearing large hoop earrings. She had been a smoker and has no teeth. She is just smiling and nodding.

A male energy coming through, his head is cocked to one side, and he has a straggly fringe. His skin appears to have acne scarring and he has teeth missing. He didn't take care of his appearance whilst on the earth plane. He admits to having mental health problems and he committed suicide. He is known to Beth, and he is smiling at her.

Another male spirit comes through. He has a fuller face and whilst he is giving us a big smile we could see his gold tooth. He indicates that he knows someone in the group. He is a large gentleman and is showing himself carrying a bit of weight. He has a double chin, moustache, blond hair thinning on top. He turns his head to show an earring in his left ear. He then leaves.

Chris

Ray Thomas, he has not been through in trance before. He tells us that he was born in Llanelli in 1899. He had joined the army and had spent time in Egypt. When he returned from Egypt he moved back to Llanelli, near Swansea. He died in 1992 aged 93. He has a daughter still on the earth-plane. He went to a care home in Burry Port and is buried in Box cemetery.

Matthew. He tells us that another group had asked him to work with them, but he had refused. He says, *'There is another small circle nearby, they have been trying to poach me to work with them – I told them to bugger off!'* He is sucking on his pipe and holding it to the right side of his mouth. We could briefly smell the tobacco. He is puffing away like mad! Ange asks about the Queen as she is very unwell. He replies, *'The end is near, preparations are being made.'* Shortly after this session the Queen did pass away. Matthew has strong opinions on certain subjects and although discussed, some of these conversations have not been documented as they may be considered controversial.

A new male spirit briefly comes through to give us healing, prayers and a blessing. He is a **Japanese Samurai.** He is chanting ME-OHM and is looking around at all of us all, nodding and smiling and acknowledging each of us but does not say anything else. He then leaves.

Gethin. He tells us, *'You are all recipients of an extraordinary healing from the Japanese Samurai, you will feel the effects very soon. We will continue to allow Matthew to come through to help develop you spiritually, but we are aware that he can overstep the mark at times. There is a process to follow in the spirit world, but Matthew does not comply with that. There is a formation and order of work.'* He tells us then that he is going to bring through some communicators.

A male spirit comes through. He has a full head of dark hair. He doesn't talk but indicates that he had had a stroke which had left him with a significant left sided weakness. He is holding his own hand and becomes very emotional. He just shows himself to us and then leaves.

Another male spirit briefly comes through then. He has a message for Paul. He tells him, *'Jason is absolutely fine. If he says that he is seeing things, there is nothing to worry about.'* He confirmed to Paul that Jason is seeing spirit.

Paul
A native American Indian comes through chanting and then says, *'Welcome, the pleasure is all mine.'* He looks around at all of us, smiling and nodding his head in turn to each of us. He tells us, *'The New Moon will bring comfort and healing to you all.'* He goes on to say that in our prayers, we must ask to find him. We thank him and he tells us that we are welcome, from him and his tribe.

Albert. Ange says, 'We've missed you.' He teases her saying that she had been talking to him earlier that day! He then tells Chris that he will take him into his classroom one day. Chris asks how quickly do the students change in his classroom? *Albert* replies, *'It is like a revolving door, there are new students coming and going all of the time.'* Chris then asks, *'How do you manage your time over there?'* **Albert** replies that he delegates his 'time' by sending his thoughts out – he says, *'Thoughts manage time.'* But he also reminds us that there is no 'time' in the spirit world, time is a man-made concept. He tells us that they are keeping a watch on what is going on in our world at this time and reminds us, *'Don't believe everything in the media, there are both positive and negative stories.* **Negative reports PROJECT FEAR***, the world is a very fearful place at the moment – there is no need to add any more fear.'* He states that we should all continue to enjoy life and plan ahead.

Chris asks, 'Does everyone in the spirit world want to learn?' **Albert** replies, *'Those that want to stay, I educate.'* He jokes *'Females want to learn everything at once!'*

Tracey asks him if her recently deceased relative had seen 'the other ones' meaning her relatives and friends, who Tracey believed had drawn close to her in her last few days on the earth plane. She explains that she had had a deep and personal communication with her just a day or two before she passed away. **Albert** reassures Tracey that her relative has acknowledged that communication with her.

Theresa asks him, 'When you teach, is it philosophical?' He replies, *'The lessons learnt on earth are usually negatives – we turn them into positives. This is what we teach. The Spirit world communicates in thoughts and colour. There is no actual language.'* **Albert** leaves then to bring some communicators through.

Colin comes through then. Someone says, 'You're putting on weight Colin.' He replies, *'Its Mam's stew!'* He tells us that he is still struggling with a bad back as he has been digging up spuds. He bent down because he thought he saw tuppence! He says he's going down the boozer tonight – *'there are pubs over here, you can't get drunk, but you can get merry.'*

PR asks Colin if he has a girlfriend in the spirit world. He replies that he doesn't have a girlfriend at the moment. He says his girlfriend on the earth-plane had been a battle-axe, and jokes that she had driven him to glue! He says that everyone has their own individual appearance but then says, about his girlfriend, *'Not her, I didn't know if I was looking at her front or her back! Only joking!'* He tells us that he does regret not having any children but states that it wouldn't have been fair as he was never there. Although it is not necessary to eat or drink in the spirit world it is still possible to do so if you want to. Colin likes to eat and drink but says that the cockles and lava-bread and bacon don't taste quite the same over there. He is enjoying spending time with his mum, dad and his nan. He was very close to his parents when he was on the earth plane and that strong bond remains.

Chow Ling. Tracey had recently given healing to Mark and she believed that she had felt *Chow Ling* draw near to her to assist her. She asks him to confirm if he had been there. He says that he had indeed joined her to assist her in Mark's healing. He says, *'Mark is very special.'* Mark confirms that he had also been aware of Chow Lings presence as he had been receiving the healing. Chow Ling invites us all to talk to him to ask for healing and knowledge.

Tracey asks how she can enhance her healing. He replies, *'The time is now to start doing medicines, learn about the herbs and leaves you can use to make tinctures and other medications. Start small, aim big, have confidence.'* He advises Tracey to make a natural healing remedy for stiff joints and tells her that he will teach her how to do this.

Again, he mentions Turmeric (Haldi) as being an invaluable root for healing.

PR has recently been experiencing a lot of stress and Chow Ling invites him to receive hands on healing from him which PR accepts with gratitude. Chow Ling chants as he gives the healing. Justine asks him if he can give mental and emotional healing as well ? **Chow Ling** replies, *'Yes, you are all welcome to ask me, but I will already know that you need healing and will be giving it to you.'*

Patrick (fishmonger) He comes through laughing in a deep voice, he is taking a lot of energy out of Paul. He jokes that he can't believe that he is working with a Chelsea fan! (Paul). He then tells Ange, Justine and Theresa that we *'can have it!'* and gets told off by Albert for being out of order. He tells us *'you can do what you want over here, you never get bored. You can play sports, bingo, cooking, even rumpy pumpy – can't wait for Theresa to come over!'* We are all laughing because he is being naughty. He tells us that Albert is holding his head in his hands in exasperation and the Shepherd's Crook is coming out! He tells us *'if you are not well travelled on the earth-plane, you can do it easily in the spirit world* *just by thinking about where you would like to go. You are there, quick as a flash.'* We are running out of time for this session now so he says goodbye for Albert to return. He tells us to *'KEEP SMILING.'*

Albert returns and says that Patrick flies close to the sun, like Icarus. Albert does not like bad language as he is a gentleman. He jokes that if Paul had a swear box he'd be skint! Albert urges Ange to *'be more disciplined and start on time'* as the time goes by really quickly in the sessions. He explains that our guides are compatible with us. They may stay with us for the whole of one lifetime but will change each lifetime. Our Guardian Angel is with us for ever. Albert says that Paul has big things coming – like celebrity – he needs us all to nurture him, which we do. Albert says that he has always guided Paul and some of the rest of us on our journeys. The paths of the individuals of the group coming together and meeting is written. **He calls us *'A Gathering of Good Souls.'*** Before he leaves, he tells us, *'**Do not let negativity influence you, it is the poison of the world. Always be in positive mind.**'* Albert has previously requested that we hold **'A Golden Ticket'** night, in which we can each invite a friend or family member to come and observe a trance session in progress. We are all very excited to do this and ask Albert when it will happen. He replies that it is up to Ange to organise it from this side, and he says that he will accommodate it and bring the appropriate souls from his side. He says that all 3 trance mediums are ready for this session.

SESSION 7
25.05.22

We are in the church/community centre. This is not our normal meeting place, but it is undergoing a re-vamp, so we have moved temporarily.

Justine

A male energy begins to come through, a huge auric field can be seen. Strong overshadowing. He has a wide nose and thin moustache and is smiling, showing his teeth. There is one tooth missing on one side.

He very quickly leaves, and a female energy comes through. Justine's head is pulled back, this female spirit has a ponytail over her left shoulder, and she is wearing glasses. She is smiling showing a distinctive gap in her teeth. There appears to be a lot of energy around the stomach area. Turning her head she looks at PR, he asks 'Is that you Mum?' She nods and smiles at him then becomes emotional.

Chris

Matthew is coming through, sucking on his pipe, we can smell sweet tobacco. He says he always used to smoke this in his pipe. He tells us that he passed away in 1967 from a heart attack, aged 82. He gives us more information about his last earth life in a later session. He talks about things that are currently going on in our world. He reminds us that we will be told things that aren't totally true by various media sources and that we must be mindful about what we believe. He says, '*DO NOT FEAR. EVERYTHING WILL BE OK. The world has been set up to give you all experiences and challenges that will help you to complete your tasks and learn.*' He tells us that he had been reprimanded by Albert for telling us things that not all members of the group are ready to hear and some of us had been a bit concerned by this. We still want Matthew to continue to work with us in our development and he promised to be more careful about the information he is giving us. He tells us that we need to focus on the **FEELINGS** we experience when considering any information we are told, also when we ask a question we should, '*FEEL THE ANSWER. LISTEN TO YOUR GUT INSTINCTS – THEY ARE ALWAYS RIGHT. REMEMBER TO SAY YOUR PRAYERS.*'

Gethin comes through strongly. He says, *'This environment (in the community centre) is absolutely fantastic.'* He goes on to say that they (Spirit) are all fully committed to working with us in any environment. He says, *'The energy is a lot stronger in this room. There will be a lot of visual and vocal experiments tonight, and there are also many other things to come.'* He leaves to bring communicators through.

Paul

White Eagle welcomes us. *'Good evening, it's a pleasure to be back. The energy is building nicely.'* He begins to chant a prayer of protection and bestows a blessing upon us. He is one of our guides for the whole group and he ensures our safety. He tells us, *'not only do you develop, so we do too.'* He is asked if he protects us outside of the group. He replies, *'Yes, there is no need to ask.'*

Tracey asks him 'How do you see us?' to which he replies, *'As human beings.'* He was asked this as other communicators have reported seeing us in different ways. Some see us as beings of coloured light or just light and others see us as more solid figures. We think this is dependent on the experience of the communicator or the level the communicator is currently at in the spirit world. He advises *us, 'Don't waste any opportunities that are given to ask questions, goodnight.'*

Albert. We tell him what we can see as he is coming through, he is always immaculately dressed and he likes us to describe what he is wearing, down to the pocket watch or glasses. He and other communicators do this to stretch our clairvoyance abilities. He is pleased at the observations and says, *'Good evening, It's nice to see the group so observant.'* He is asked what kind of dwelling does he live in? He replies that he lives in dorms (Dormitories) such as he did when he was in Oxford University in his last earth-life.

Ange asks if, while on the earth plane you experience a lack of money, is there opportunity in the spirit world to have money? Albert *replies, 'Yes, but everyone is equal. When the soul leaves the earth plane and crosses the bridge, we are taught that material things no longer matter.'* He says that we as human beings are all materialistic in varying degrees. He says, *'It has been a common theme today with The Boy.'* Paul had been out shopping today, unaware that

Albert had been with him. He reminds us *'You can't take it with you.* **LIVE YOUR LIFE WITH NO REGRETS.'**

PR asks if his parents are now together in the spirit world. Albert replies, *'Yes they are, you will know if they come back to visit you.'* Albert tells PR that he has lots of stuff to sort out following the passing over of his father, he needs to find something important. His parents have taken over guardianship of Nancy Boy (Ange and Pete's cat, who has also recently passed over the rainbow bridge). Albert tells us, *'Do not weep for any souls, they are far better looked after over here.'* To PR he says, *'Your uncle and grandmother are also with your parents. Your father was very disappointed that his tractor wasn't there!'*

We ask Albert questions about our own guides and helpers, and he tells us that we need to ask our guides to come forward in the trance sessions, so that we can see them and speak to them. He reminds us that they see and hear everything that we say, think and do anyway – nothing goes unnoticed. They are just waiting for us to ask them for their help, guidance and protection and they will be delighted to oblige. All of us human beings have guides, helpers and Guardian Angels who are with us constantly, but they cannot do anything without us asking them to because we have free will. We must choose to seek their help.

Colin. He comes through complaining, *'They want me to play rugby see!'* He explains that the Welsh rugby team in spirit want him to play prop, but he says that he is knackered doing his garden. He still hasn't got his teeth in and tells us that he doesn't like wearing them as he's not used to having teeth! Colin says to *PR, 'Oh, he's back again!'*

Tracey asks if we can still have sex in the spirit world? Colin says, *'Yes, and it's much better than sex on the earth-plane!'* He says that he was happiest when he was at his biggest and fittest on the earth-plane, but his back had been bad. He jokes *'Paul's back is bad from carrying his wallet!'* He loves to moan as it gets him sympathy.

Tracey then asks, 'Do we look the same in the Spirit world?' Colin replies, *'You can look how you want. You have a lot to learn – but don't forget that teaching is a two-way thing.'* He explains that when we return to the spirit world, we will teach others and we will be asked why we had done the things that we did whilst on the earth plane. He jokes that he put the engine of his Ford Cortina in backwards on the earth plane and asks himself, *'Why did I do that?'* He reminds us, *'You have got to live your life. Enjoy every moment because it is over very quickly.'* In the spirit world he lives with his parents in a council house with a garden, a greenhouse, and a garage at the bottom of the garden. He had created his home in his mind. It is a replica of the house he used to live in on the earth plane. He was used to it and comfortable in it.

Master Long. He is Justine's guide. Albert had brought him through because she had asked to meet one of her guides. He is a Tibetan monk (Holy Man). He tells her that he *'guides and protects her.'* He says that he prays for her and asks her to meditate with him. He says there are many guides waiting – when we need them, they will come. He reassures us, saying, *'your guides are never absent whether you want them or not.'* He is smiling gently. Before he leaves, he turns to Ange and tells her, *'Your vision is exceptional.'*

Iestyn Thomas. He is from Swansea, he passed away in 1996, aged 67. He had suffered a massive stroke which had left his speech affected. He had worked in a private mine. He didn't give us any more information about himself but says that the reason for him coming through is because he was asked to – but he was having difficulty adjusting the energies enough to come through stronger. He tells us that 'they' (spirit) are giving him *'a little minute, just to see it for himself.'* He is very thankful for the opportunity. He tells us that *'there is a massive queue waiting.'* He goes then as his wife is making his tea. He is having boiled potatoes. He says, *'Lovely meeting you all, Goodnight.'* We tell him that it was lovely to meet him too and invite him to come through again.

Albert returns. He says, *'Your guides are waiting. Send thoughts out to them in the forthcoming weeks.'* He tells us that they want us to use our other senses to develop comprehensively.

Tracey asks if the lovely lady that was assisting her in healing that week was a Holy Lady. Albert wouldn't answer but told her to go with her gut feeling.

SESSION 8
22.06.22

Justine

Immediate strong overshadowing -there is a male spirit coming through. He has a moustache and a goatee-style beard, a wide nose which looks like it may have been broken at some point. He has got black hair and appears to be about 50 years of age. He is smiling and looking around.

An older female spirit comes through next. She appears to have false teeth as they look too perfect to be her own. She has dark curly hair cut into a bob and is carrying a bit of weight. Ange gets the impression that she would have been a very hard worker in her last life, and she thinks that she had been a cockle picker. When asked this she indicates that the information is correct.

A younger female spirit comes through then. She has ginger hair and is wearing large glasses. She is looking around and smiling at everyone.

Then another male energy shows himself quickly, he has long sideburns and a moustache and is wearing a bandana. He just came and went, just *'popped'* in to see what was going on.

Chris
An Oriental gentleman. He has small features, very prominent eyes which are wide open, he is staring at us and gesturing with his hands. He is chanting and giving us all a blessing. We thank him for the blessing, and he leaves.

Matthew comes through, he is sucking hard on his pipe. He tells us that he has 2 novices working with him tonight. He has been disciplined by Albert for telling us things that had upset a couple of us in the group as he is so forthright. He is allowed to meet with us so long as he is seen to be spiritually developing us. He says, *'We are working together* (his group and Gethin's group) *in agreement to develop you.'* Gethin's group and Albert are concerned that Matthew is rushing this opportunity. Consequently, he is being limited to what he can say, and he must prove to Albert and Gethin that he has an agenda for our development. This is to enhance all of our senses. He tells us that he will show us the meanings of colours that show illness or injury in the physical body. Mark tells Matthew that he can already see these colours as he is a healer. He shows us his right shoulder and asks us what we can see. We tell him that it looks as if it had been dislocated. He is showing us this to test our clairvoyant abilities. This had happened to him whilst he had been on the earth-plane, and he describes it as being very painful. Of course he is completely fine now. There is no pain in the spirit world. Before he leaves, he tells us that, *'There are very good things to come for us and you.'* This is very encouraging for us, and we thank him for continuing to work with us.

An older female spirit briefly comes through, she tells us that she was taken ill on a beach whilst she was on holiday. She had been sitting on a deck chair on the beach at the time. She didn't pass away there but was taken to hospital where she did then die. She was a bit of a character and large as life. She didn't stay for long but was very grateful for the opportunity to come through.

Paul

Beth's father-in-law briefly shows himself to us but doesn't speak. She was pleased that he had taken the time to come through.

One of her guides named **Gorat** comes through. He tells her *'It's a pleasure to meet you, you must keep lighting the candle.'* Beth does that every day when she is praying. He says, *'You must learn to trust Beth, you will block your own development otherwise.'* Gorat tells us that he had lived in Nepal. He had been a monk and he had had many brothers (other monks). He explains that so far, he has only lived once on the earth-plane and one day he will reincarnate. He is not in any rush to do that yet. He says, *'I will come when the world is a better place to inhabit.'* He tells us, *'there are so many people waiting to come through. The queue goes back further than the eye can see.'* He leaves to allow other communicators to come through.

Albert. Ange says, 'Its lovely to see you Albert, it seems so long.' Albert replies, *'You were only speaking to me this afternoon!'* Alberts moustache is pointing upwards at both ends tonight. He tells us that he no longer considers us students, but as friends. Ange tells him that she can't wait to get her new dog and he says that he has been watching her looking at the pictures of the dog on her phone. Ange asks about a young man who fell to his death off a building site recently. Albert says that *'he had experienced some difficulty at his passing as it had been so sudden. It was a shock to him, but he has been received. Many people who suffer traumatic injuries appear to have a stronger spiritual self on recovery.'* Ange says that she has had many different experiences in the spirit world, and asks, 'When someone has an out-of-body experience but has to return to the body, is it because they were not expected in the spirit world?' Albert replies reassuringly, *'No, it is because it is not their time to die.'*

Mark says that he is fascinated by spirit moving things (Apporting). Albert says, *'The energy it takes to move something is tremendous, but it certainly does happen, eg: moving tables, moving objects, sometimes from one room to another. They* (spirit) *think it's funny! Most of the time they do it to try to get your attention, to let you know that they are still there.'*

Colin. He tells us that he has been in the greenhouse all day, tending to his strawberries. He says that he always grows strawberries when the tennis is on! He asks where 'blondie' (Theresa) is as she's not there. Ange jokes 'Have you gone off me now?' Colin replies, *'I'm not allowed – he's here!'*

He is referring to PR, who is Ange's husband. Colin says to PR *'It's nice to see you smile after all that you've been through recently, you've been through the mill. There is a lot of support for you spirit side.'* Ange asks Colin 'When we are not in group, do you look in on us?' Colin replies, *'No, too busy growing strawberries!'* He tells us that he is looking for a girlfriend. Ange says, 'Can you change your looks?' Colin pretends to be offended and replies, *'What are you trying to say?'*

Colin tells us that next time he comes through he is going to bring along a mate who has died suddenly. He explains, *'He's come over suddenly but is with his mum and dad now.'* Colin jokes to PR, *'Don't make any plans for next week!'* and gets told off by Albert for making a joke about death!

Chow Ling. He tells Tracey that she needs a 'recharge.' She thanks him for helping her with the healing sessions that she and Mark hold in the Spiritualist church. Chow Ling chants and hums very loudly as he gives us all healing. He asks us to say the colour that we see when we feel the energy. This is a test. He then puts his hand on Tracey's shoulder and works on that as she had been experiencing pain and discomfort there recently.

Albert returns – PR asks about a recent television programme he saw on a former celebrity, that had been proven to have committed sexual assaults on young people – a Faking It special. He asks, 'Where has he gone?' Albert tells us *'He and people like him go to the lower realms. There are many people like it but in the spirit world it is seen as an illness in comparison to it being seen as a crime* here (on the earth-plane.) *They are shown the error of their ways and have to make amends.'*

Rob asks, 'Is there any advice you can give The Boy regarding the upcoming service in church?' (Paul is due to be giving a demonstration of mediumship on the platform in the forthcoming week.) Albert replies encouragingly, *'The Boy will be fine.'* Albert promises that he will be there with The Boy, Chris and Rob for the service. He says that Paul has been bombarded from the spirit world in the last few weeks as he had been absent from the group. He goes on to say that Paul knew he had to come back to group, he couldn't resist the draw any longer. He is pleased to say that Paul is so much more positive now.

Mark asks Albert for advice on the direction of his spiritual path. Albert tells Mark that he is trying to juggle too many balls. He says, *'Stop juggling all the balls and prioritise the ones which are most important to you, for example your family, relationships, spiritual work, job etc and concentrate on those.'* He tells Mark that he currently has 5 balls in the air to juggle and advises him, *'you cannot juggle 100. Your guides will juggle some of them for you, but you must stick to 5.'* He goes on to tell Mark that he is a fantastic healer. He is being pushed forward by Ange – she has added 1 ball, but it is one of the five. Mark is also receiving help from another guide. This guide comes through briefly and acknowledges Mark.

SESSION 9
06.07.22

Justine

A male spirit is coming through, he has dark circles under his eyes and a moustache. He is wearing gold-coloured glasses on the end of his nose, and he has a gold tooth which is glinting in the light. He is smiling and nodding as he is looking around but leaves then to allow other communicators to come through.

A young female spirit comes through. She has black hair or it is tied back. She indicates that she knows someone in the room. Paul recognises her, it is his cousin **Michelle.** Paul asks, 'are you with Nan'? She nods yes to confirm that she is. She is smiling as Paul relays a story from their childhood in which he had locked her in the garden shed. She tells Paul that she was glad to be released from her earthly body as she had been very ill. Paul is quite emotional at this, but he is very happy that she has come through.

Chris

Gethin comes through and says, *'There are different forces at play, there will be two groups working with Chris.'* He explains that one is Gethin's group, the other is Matthew's group. They have come to a mutual agreement for both of their groups to work together for the benefit of our spiritual development, but they have different agendas and different methods of teaching and advising us.

A male spirit comes through for Our Pete. He tells Our Pete to listen to him for everything, he promises that he will help and guide him. He places his hand onto his chest to show his love for Pete and says, *'Love to you.'* Our Pete is unsure if he recognises him but accepts the message and is very grateful.

Matthew. He is sucking hard on his pipe – the smell of Old Holborn tobacco is noticeable. He admits that he had suffered with a bad chest in life but wouldn't give up his pipe! He tells us that he is very grateful for the opportunities he is being given to come through and speak to us. He *says, 'Mediums such as Chris and Paul are very few and far between, we* (spirit) *don't get many chances to work like* *this.'* Matthew asks us to describe what he is wearing. Many of the communicators ask us to describe their physical appearance and the clothes that they are wearing and any other items they would have used on the earth-plane, such as a walking stick. It is to help strengthen our clairvoyant abilities. Rob tells him that he sees him wearing a tartan coat and a monocle and chain, Matthew confirms this and compliments Rob saying that he has *'excellent power.'* Before he goes, he says, *'The world is in great turmoil, there are wars and uncertainty, great hardship, inequality, suffering and famine and drought.* ***IT IS ALL DOWN TO GREED, POLITICS AND RELIGION AS USUAL.'*** He tells us not to lose hope.

Paul

Aram comes through, he tells us that he is Egyptian and is one of Justine's guides. He helps her with trance. He appears young and is wearing a robe. He has a beard and moustache and curly hair. Chris says that he looks like Jesus. He informs us that he is Royalty, and that Justine was his sister in a past life. He tells her that *'our family were healers'* He tells her to *'Keep looking for our colour'* – which is orange. Justine states that she had seen the colour orange around his head, and he confirmed she was correct. He says, *'Now that you are embraced, your path will follow easier.* **PEACE BE WITH YOU ALL'.** He reminds Justine to think of him when she is doing trance.

Albert. Ange has brought her little dog Freya to meet us all. Albert jokes *'Lovely to see the little dog here, I hope she does not have fleas!'* Ange says that there are only a few of us there tonight as trance was unexpected. Albert replies, *'It was not unexpected at all, and that only a few makes no difference to this group.'*

Chris asks why does he now have two spirit groups (Gethin and Matthew) working with him? Albert replies, *'It is a bit of a taboo subject over here, the two groups work differently.'* He goes on to say that whilst he is all for us being aware of the troubles currently occurring on the earth-plane, not everyone in the group wants to know as it may upset them. *'Spirit picks up the hesitancy from those who prefer not to know.'*

Albert praises Rob, Chris and Paul for the service they had delivered in a spiritualist church on the Sunday before this trance session. Albert had recognised that Paul was struggling with his confidence a bit because of audience negativity. He tells us, *'The whole thing was a test.'* but goes on to say, *'The Boy did very well, and even wrote a poem, which we* (spirit) *helped him with.'* He tells Ange that Freya is here to help her. He says, *'She was put into your heart for a reason.'* The reason becomes apparent a while later.

Rob's friend and former co-worker **John** comes through. He advises Rob, *'Be more confident in everything you do, and pay more attention when you're driving!'* He jokes *'work is a loose word with Rob, I know because I used to work with him!'* Rob's former occupation was as a butcher in Swansea Market. John says that Rob always wanted to do better and confirms to Rob, *'You made the right decision to leave that job.'* Rob says that John had been a good boss and always a friend. John returns the compliment, saying, *'there was nothing not to like about Rob, he could sell meat to all the ladies – young or old!.'* Rob says to John that he will tell Brian that John has come through *'just to see his face!'* John replies, *'You'd better make sure he's sitting down first.'* As he's leaving, he says to us all, *'Nice to see you all.'*

Colin. He says to Ange *'OMG – you've traded him* (her husband PR) *in for a dog! Don't show her to The Boy, he'll use her as a fly on his fishing rod!'* (Freya is a very fluffy dog!) Colin says that he had been sitting listening to us chatting earlier in the evening when we had been discussing the current troubles going on in the world. He advises us not to ask him for his opinion and jokes *'I'm thick as s**t! I don't know what's going to happen and I'm not educated enough to say anything anyway.'* He praises Paul's mediumship, saying *'The Boy is doing REALLY well.'*

We tell Colin that we always love to speak to him, he always makes us laugh even when he's trying to say something serious! He tells us that we've all got to smile and show our teeth. He jokes *'You're lucky you've got them!'*

Albert returns. He tells Justine that they are going to start using her voice very soon, they are manipulating her voice box. He warns us *'Your kin will endure some societal pain.* **'STAY STRONG, KEEP YOUR BELIEF.** *You must remember it's all about education and evolution. The technology now is what drives the man – it evolves. The same controllers are the same controllers – GREED AND POWER*

*– There has always been greed, it powers all. It will never be eradicated. Things **will** get better. EMBRACE YOUR FREEDOM.'* Before he leaves Albert says that he wishes people could see the evil in the world. *'The minority spoils it for the majority. Look after yourselves, mentally and physically, your guides are there – 10 deep for each of you. Paul will get his wish – it will be life changing for him,* (he wishes to open a healing centre). *His belief is paramount.* **MANIFEST EVERYTHING – IT WILL HAPPEN!.'**

SESSION 10
13.07.22

Justine

Her head has been pulled right back, there is an old man coming through. He has a moustache and his hair is thinning on top. There is shading on bridge of his nose. He indicates that he had travelled extensively with his job, and he has been in spirit for a long time.

    A female spirit comes through then. She has a small face and blonde bobbed hair. She indicates that she had suffered with thyroid and stomach problems but had passed away through a cancerous condition. She had run a social club and had been a barmaid. She liked bingo and karaoke and was an organiser involved with the running of the club.

    Paul says that he feels the reason for Justine not yet speaking is because they are still testing our clairvoyance skills. (Her voice box is not being manipulated by spirit yet).

Paul

***A Native American Indian* comes through** – he is chanting, then says, *'Good evening. I have come in peace and solitude. I welcome your questions.'*

Our Pete asks a question about healing. Our Pete has exceptional healing ability but is not currently practicing his gift. He replies, *'Healing is the highest of energies, through the guides, it is a gift that just keeps giving. You* (Our Pete) *are at a level you feel comfortable with. You need to be pushed.'*

Ange sometimes says that she can't wait to be 'over there'. He tells her *'Do not wish your life away. You are needed. You were sent back to fight the negativity. Your teaching is important around the world. You were all sent back to fight the negativity that exists in your world today.'*

Justine asks if she had been a native American Indian in a past life as she felt that she had a strong connection with them. He told us that Our guides will decide if we are to be shown our past lives but does confirm that Justine was once part of his tribe.

A new male spirit comes through. He has a prominent scar down the left side of his face. We can see that the left side of his face is drooping, and Ange could see that he had a cleft palate to his tongue, he confirms this. He says, 'My name is **Robert Emmanuel the Third.** *I lived in Westminster, London and I worked as an investigative journalist for the Times newspaper. I was born in 1768 and died in 1843, aged 75 years. I enjoyed a good life.'* He tells us he had been classed as an unusual reporter because he had always reported **THE TRUTH.** In efforts to discredit his writings, he had been described as a saboteur by those people who held positions of responsibility and power, as they didn't want their personal and private businesses reported on for the whole world to see. He was attacked with a broken glass as a threat, and this had caused the large scar down the left side of his face. He says, *'Nevertheless, I maintained my beliefs and continued to report on the subjects that other journalists would not.'*

Theresa asks if he had reported on the workhouses. He replies, *'Yes, many of them.'* He tells us that he believes that he is needed in our group, and he is welcomed by us all. He states, *'Nothing has changed on the earth plane since I* was alive, except technology. Technology has evolved to shape the world and it will continue to evolve.'

Ange asks why can't people who reincarnate do something about the state of the world? Robert replies, *'They don't remember the spirit world when they come back to the earth-plane, their spiritual knowledge is erased for the time-period of that new life.'* We ask him if he has thought of returning to the earth-plane. He says that he has not yet reincarnated but says, *'When planning our new lives with our guides, we have some input into the decisions made, but can't change most of what will come, as Karmic Debt always needs to be repaid. Your world revolves around MONEY. GREED AND POWER WANT MORE GREED AND POWER, AND LIES SELL.'* He reminds us that not everyone tells us the truth, and to question everything that we see, hear and read, and take nothing for granted. He says, *'Bad people are not born bad, they have free will. This gives them choice, to be a good person or to become a bad person. For example, by committing crimes. When bad people pass over into the spirit world they are sent straight back to the earth plane without a choice. They MUST reincarnate. They will then experience the types of crimes committed to them as they had* *previously done to others in their last life. They must decide on how they will **react**, this will be a task.'*

When asked what he thought about our trance sessions he says, *'It is a wonderful opportunity for us as it is very easy for spirit people to transition into someone in trance.'* He then tells us that he will speak to us regularly. He says to look closely around his head as he tries to show us an item of clothing. Rob says he sees a bowler hat and Robert tells him that he is correct.

Albert returns briefly to advise us that if we ever feel a blockage when we are linking in with spirit, it is because a new guide is coming through to work with us. He jokingly tells us off for forgetting our homework (we were all supposed to be thinking of questions to ask him, but none of us had!) He asks Ange to arrange another Q+A session as the last session had been very interesting for both sides.

A new female guide comes through for Tracey. She is a very old Japanese lady, her name is **XZY (pronounced SHY)**, She is singing beautifully. She tells us that she used to live in the mountains in Japan, where it was very cold. She was a medicine woman and healer and people used to walk for miles to come to see her. She holds Tracey's hands and says to her, *'You are a medicine woman too. You are very special.'* She encourages Tracey to start looking into herbal medicine and build on her healing abilities.

A New male spirit. He tells us his name is **Paddy.** He describes himself as an Irish tinker. He died in 1987 of cancer. Ange whispers to us 'He's got big ears!' He responds by saying *'Cheeky'* and telling Ange that she's got big boobs! We all laugh as it's so funny to hear the spirits speak as they would have done on the earth-plane. He says his family and friends are Romany gypsies and they used to go into a shop where Ange had worked. On the earth-plane he had lived in a caravan and had loved it, that was his way of life. But he states, *'Gypsies and travellers are a very misunderstood bunch and are always getting persecuted by the police. They have a right to travel just like everyone else.'* He then jokes, *'But if it's not pinned down, we'll take it!'* He tells Ange that she has a female gypsy guide and jokes that it could even be his wife as *'she gets around everywhere!'* Ange says that she has just seen a blue light by him, and he jokes, *'I haven't* *nicked the gates over here yet! It would be just my luck (luck of the Irish) to reincarnate back into a policeman!'* He tells Ange that the next time she sees his relatives, he will be standing beside her.

Albert returns. He tells us that Justine and Theresa will soon be doing platform work. He tells Ange to take little steps with us, but she must also push us. Albert will join us on the platform.

SESSION 11
03.08.22

<u>Justine</u>

Immediate very strong overshadowing. There is a young female spirit coming through, she is smiling broadly and appears very serene. She is moving her mouth as if trying to speak.

She quickly fades away, then an older female comes through. She appears to be 40-50 years old with a full face and dishevelled dark hair. Again, she fades away quickly. Spirit is bringing in communicators quickly to test the mediums clairvoyance abilities.

A male spirit comes through, he has a moustache and a very distinctive nose upon which a pair of glasses are perched. He is smiling, proudly showing us his gold tooth. We recognise him as he has been through before.

Another female spirit comes through. She has curly bobbed hair and she has a right sided facial droop suggesting a stroke. Her name is ***Jennifer,*** she died aged 38. She is one of Ange's friends. Ange hugs Jen (Justine) and she becomes very emotional. Ange tells her that she thinks of her every day. Jen had suffered a major stroke and was left wheelchair bound. A second massive stroke took her over to the spirit world.

Chris

***Matthew* comes through -** He tells us that this evening there will be visual experiments and then time for questions. He asks us to describe what he is wearing. Rob says that he sees him smoking a pipe which looked like the type of pipe Sherlock Holmes would use in the movies. We can see that the fingers he uses to hold his pipe are glowing green. He also says that Matthew is wearing a chequered jacket. Matthew confirms that he is correct. He has 4 members of his group working with him this evening. We are all seeing more colours and the shapes of other communicators around the mediums in the box. We discuss what is going on in the world currently, then Matthew leaves to allow other communicators to come through.

A new male spirit - Oriental gentleman – he has come in to lift the energy as it had dropped following the conversations with Matthew. The energies can drop if we are tired or if we are worried or upset about anything. We are blessed to have a few communicators, including Colin, who come through to make us laugh – laughter raises the vibrations and the energy. The energy has to be high to facilitate the communicators to come through and to communicate clearly, otherwise they can struggle to speak to us. This gentleman is a very powerful energy, he begins to send out healing energy to us. There is a bright orange colour emanating from both of his hands. He is lifting his hands up, palms facing upwards, then bringing them down forcefully with his palms facing down. He is also chanting a powerful blessing. We are very grateful for this upliftment and blessing and we thank him for coming through.

A new male spirit – A young gentleman comes through. Albert has given him permission to come through as he is one of Albert's students. He tells us that he has come on Albert's behalf, purely as an experiment. He thanks us for this opportunity and tells us that he thinks it is fascinating. He says, *'My name is **Edward May**, I was 19 years old when I passed over to the spirit world. I died from complications of my appendix in 1847. You all have family and friends* *sitting all around you, they are watching and enjoying this trance session.'* We ask him how we appear to him and he replies that he sees us as beings of light. He says, *'As I develop in class under Albert's guidance, I will begin to see you as solid human beings.'* He tells us that when he graduates from Albert's class, he would like to help us develop as a group. He thinks he can make a difference from what he has learnt from Albert. He says that he will tell us things that we have never heard before (but still under Albert's supervision). Before he goes he says, *'God bless you all.'*

Paul

A new male spirit – He says, *'Good evening, my name is* **MEEART***, peace be with you all.'* He isn't anyone's guide but has also come through to lift the energies. We can see that he is wearing robes and he has deep grooves in his face. He says, **'They call me the caretaker.'** He helps all those in the spirit world but doesn't say exactly how. We assume that he holds a similar position to Albert as Albert is also called a caretaker. He says that his ancestry dates back to 1306. He had lived in Lebanon and he had been a foot soldier. Chris feels a strong connection and a bond of love with Meeart. He tells Chris that they were both soldiers in the same battle in 1384. At that time Chris's name had been **MYRAM**. Meeart compliments Chris, saying that he (MYRAM) was a true warrior. It was the only life that he has shared with Chris. Before he leaves he says sadly, *'persecution will never go away.'*

Albert comes in and tells us all to settle down (very professor-like!) as he says we were all chatting like noisy schoolchildren. He pretends to be exasperated with us and says that we have all chewed his ears off over the last couple of weeks! We have all got into the habit of sending our thoughts to Albert instead of our own guides. He reminds us to ask our own guides and helpers for guidance, support and protection, but says with fondness that he always thinks of us too and looks in on us from time to time.

    Ange asks why Edward May can only see us as light coloured beings when Albert can see us as human beings as plain as day. Albert replies that there is ongoing training for them in the spirit world to enable them to see us as human beings.

Justine says, 'In trance, Paul goes into your classroom, Chris steps to one side, what do I need to do or focus on so that my thoughts will not interfere with the spirit communicating? Can my guides take me away from the communication?' Albert replies, *'Yes, your guides can take you out to distract your attention. Also, when you meditate, focus on a classroom clock. Remember that you are new to this, trance is your speciality but no matter how safe or confident you feel, any doubt that enters your thoughts will result in your guides moving back. It will happen in the right time and it will be great.'*

Theresa asks if a human being can reincarnate into an animal such as a dog. Albert replies, *'You will come back as yourself, animals stay as animals.'* He jokes, *'The Boy would like to come back as a fish!'* (The Boy is an avid angler who eats, sleeps and breathes fishing.) Theresa then says, 'There appears to be an increase in interest from young people in alternative and complementary therapies including crystals and other methods of healing, is this just a coincidence or has there been assistance from spirit?' Albert *replies, 'With crystals and the healing processes there will always be input and inspiration from spirit. It is a natural process and young people are becoming more spiritual and aware. This is to be encouraged.'*

Beth asks, 'Why do people fight against each other in religious wars when we all believe in the same Great Spirit?' Albert replies, **'Religion is the myth of the war, we have ONE GREAT SPIRIT. Religion is blamed as an excuse for GREED. The Almighty does not want war, so why would He invent religion to do that? Religion is a man-made concept.'**

A new male Spirit – Ling Lau. He is a monk. We can see that he has big ears and some of his teeth are missing. He is laughing at this observation and says, *'Thank you.'* He tells us all (meaning all humanity) that we have many lessons to learn.

Rob asks, 'Is there a price to pay for having readings instead of trusting in the spirit realms to guide us?' Ling Lau answers *'Trust and obey, no price to pay. We choose our path.'* He goes on to say that Rob leads the path for many, reminding him that, *'Trust is paramount to be a good leader.'* Ling Lau tells us he thinks that we talk funny on the earth plane, and he finds that highly amusing.

Colin. He comes in very briefly. We ask how he is doing this week. He says, *'I'm bloody brand new!'* He teases Chris saying that one day he is going to step into him! He jokes *'He won't know what's happening!'* He tells us that Albert is going to allow him to play this trick.

Albert returns He says, *'The Boy has asked about my colleagues, they are **Ambassadors** and they have come from the **Higher Realms. They are called The Legion.** They often disguise themselves but they are really highly intellectual beings. They want to come and meet you all too. They will come through to you soon.'*

Beth asks Albert, 'Can a spirit come back to the same family they were a member of in their last life?' Albert says, *'No, everyone gets reborn into a new life with counselling and guidance from their guides.'* He goes on to say to us all**,** *'Stop thinking about past and future as you can't do anything about them. Look back and reminisce, look forward and HOPE. CONCENTRATE ON NOW.'*

This question is asked: 'What is happening to our world?' Albert advises *'You need to take financial precautions. Do not put all of your finances under the mattress*. *LEAVE IT IN THE BANK. DIGITAL CURRENCY WILL BE THE NORM IN 5 YEARS.* *Innovation and technology are always moving on*. **YOU MUST ENJOY EVERYDAY LIFE NOW, DON'T WORRY.'**

Another question: 'Are we going to be controlled to the extent that some people are by their governments?' Albert replies, *'No, but there is control to some extent already. Think about it, you are controlled at every stage of your life, in all of your normal day to day activities by Laws and Acts, rules and regulations. They are in place for many reasons – GOOD and BAD.* **GOOD THINGS WILL COME. EMBRACE THE FUTURE, WHAT HAPPENS, HAPPENS. EMBRACE IT ALL. LOOK TO THE NOW.'**

We say goodbye to Albert then, and tell him we look forward to seeing him again very soon.

SESSION 12
24.08.22

Paul

White Eagle is chanting a prayer and a blessing. He welcomes us. He tells Tracey and Justine that he was aware of them talking about him earlier when they were driving down to Llanelli. He says, *'Numbers are low tonight (in group) but it makes no difference.'*

Tracey asks him, 'Is there such a thing as a soul shepherd? Do they retrieve lost souls to go into the light?' White Eagle replies, *'Yes, they are known as GUARDIANS. THE POWER OF PRAYER HELPS, ALL GO INTO THE LIGHT.'* (This is discussed again in a later trance session.)

Albert. Ange wants to know if who she will reincarnate into is written in the Akashic records. Albert confirms that **everything** is written in the Akashic records, but he doesn't know who she will become in her next incarnation. He says, *'You will all have access to these records when you return to the spirit world, so you can read the plans then. All lessons that need to be learnt will be written in them.'*

Albert tells us that his parents were part of the metaphysical movement when he was a young man, but he was more interested in books. He jokes, *'that interest in books is not replicated in The Boy.'* He goes on to say *'perhaps this is not such a bad thing as you now have such wonderful technology. However, taking the manual techniques out of using equipment that you would have used before (eg: a typewriter) stops you thinking properly.'* He advises us to think logically and says, *'To get any information into someone you must TEACH them.* **DISCIPLINE IS THE KEY. Healing and teaching are of the highest order.'**

Tracey asks, 'What made you select The Boy to work with you?' Albert replies that Paul was brought to the group as his legacy was to be brought to spirit. He reminds us again that everything is written, and that spirit has been with us all for years, and the fact that we are all here together now is no coincidence.

Theresa asks whether fairies and other elementals really exist. Albert replies, *'There are beings called fairies – these are normal beings in a different way. They are* childlike. Everyone has an inner child, and we need to let them out now and then.'

Colin. He comes through briefly, saying, *'I've heard it all now – bloody fairies!'* Ange asks him if he sees fairies and he jokes *'Yes – when I was on the glue love! If anyone walked in here now, they'd think we were all on the glue!'* For anyone unwittingly walking into the community centre when we are sitting for trance, they would see us all sitting in the dark, the medium sitting in a large black box, wearing a black cape, with a red light focussed on the medium's face. It would look like a floating head in a box! Before he goes, Colin jokes that he was going to fart and gets told off by Albert!

A new male spirit – Aneurin Williams. He says, *'I should not have died. I was only 52 when I passed.'* He tells us that he was killed in 1983 when he was a passenger in a car being driven by a drunk driver. He acknowledges that he was silly to get into the car as he had known that the driver was drunk. He now accepts that it was his time to return to the spirit world, but it had hit him like a tonne of bricks. He asks, *'Is* *my nose straight?'* Bless him. He had hit the dashboard face on. He says, *'I want to reincarnate but I am having a bit of learning here first.'* He says that he can't settle in the spirit world. The driver is now in his 80s and still carries the blame. Aneurin's brother still lives in the Welsh village they were born in. He tells us he liked to have a couple of pints after work but advises us to stay away from drunk drivers. He says, *'One drink is one too many.'*

Albert returns – He tells us to *'Keep spreading the word about the existence of the afterlife and the power of love and positivity.'* We are the only group that keeps a journal (which is becoming this book). Albert is delighted that we do.

He reminds us, *'The spirit world is the **REALITY** – earth life is an illusion, but it is a series of necessary tasks and learnings that must be completed/achieved. There are many other planes of existence including other earth type planets identical to yours, which are also schools of learning. There are not just human souls in your world, and there are beings who are not nice beings.'* He reassures us that we all have eternal souls, but those unpleasant souls don't. Albert describes these beings as *'dead'* and gets told off for using that word, so he changed that word to *'other species'*. He describes them as being *'the lowest of the low, they disguise themselves as human beings to enable them to gain your trust.'* Albert advises us to ask Robert Emmanuel the 3rd about these beings, as he is best informed to answer our questions.

Albert says that he sees us in 20 years still together as a group. Tracey tells him that she had a very vivid impression on waking up, that she was holding a new baby. What did that mean? Albert tells her *'good news is on the horizon,'* and jokes that it will not be her getting pregnant! He tells us that our guides hear all the questions we ask him, and they give him the advice to pass onto us. He tells us *'Every one of you brings something wonderful to the group, and the spirit world is very grateful for your dedication and commitment.'*

Beth says that she woke up at 1.11 am the other day as she could hear someone dribbling a ball. Albert tells her that it is the son she miscarried, he is with her sister and father in spirit. The little boy is intrigued with life at Beth's home and he feels secure there with them. Her other son hears the ball too. Before he leaves, Albert wishes us all, *'Be blessed and goodnight.'*

SESSION 13
21.09.22

Justine

A young male comes through. He has a moustache, stubble on his chin, chubby cheeks and is smiling. He turns his head and is showing us an injury he had sustained to the left side of his face. He has long dark hair with a fringe. He has been through before and is known to Beth. He had been addicted to drugs and alcohol and had suffered with poor mental health. Rob picks up on him thinking, *'Wow, I can't believe I can hear and see you all – it's beyond what I imagined.'*

An older female comes through – she has a full face, and her hair is a permed bob, her fringe is dyed. She has large dark eyes and looks very serene. Rob feels that she was often alone in her later days. She had one son, but they were not close, and he had moved away. Her husband was not around either. She gives us the name Stephen.

Another female comes through quickly – she has pink in her hair (she looked like a punk), she is wearing glasses and has a piercing to her right ear. She had suffered an unpleasant passing but didn't give any details.

Ange explained that these new spirit contacts faded away quickly due to their inexperience of coming through. Justine says that she felt that she had gone deeper this time.

Rob

There is a glowing turquoise light evident over Rob's left shoulder and around his neck. A male spirit is coming through. (Ange could sense a lot of tension in Rob and told him to relax as he is blocking the energy). There appears to be some swelling or a mark to the centre of his forehead and there is a tear running down Rob's right cheek. He is very emotional and overwhelmed and is struggling to speak. He tells himself to 'get a bit of composure.' The male spirit finally blends the energies to allow him to speak. He says, *'It's an absolute pleasure to be invited to join you and distinguished spirit guests. My name is Duncan.'* He is amazed at coming through and says, *'It's incredible!'*

He tells us that Albert had invited him to come along this evening as he had come through in the last trance session briefly but hadn't spoken. He says, *'I was a squadron leader in the RAF in WW2. I was based at an airfield near Dover, and I was shot down in battle over the sea. We were set up there as a rapid response, we lost many chaps.'* He tells us that he spends a lot of time in the spirit world working with other air-force personnel, to receive newly passed personnel and help them to adjust, to settle in. He says, *'Some struggle to come to terms with the fact that they have passed over, especially young men who had their whole lives in front of them.'*

Duncan states that he chose to do this job in the spirit world as it helps him to feel useful. He says, *'When they have adjusted, many go into Alberts class. They have certain skills such as RAF intelligence.'* Duncan describes Albert as a *'frightfully nice chap.'* He tells us that it took a lot of effort to blend with Rob tonight as Rob was tense and struggling to relax. He goes on to say that although he and Rob had met once before in a previous trance session, it was different this time. He tells Rob, *'Please relax and try to enjoy the journey – we are ok. It's important to enjoy every encounter and make the most of it and of opportunities that come our way. Don't focus on negativity, it drags you down – then you will miss the joys of life. These words are given with so much love from the spirit world from our learned friends. If there is something negative in your life – step away from it and let it pass you by.'* These are very wise and heart-felt words which we all would benefit from by putting them into practice in our own lives. These words highlight the message and the purpose of this book.

A new spirit – older male, he says to Our Pete that he is from Ropewalk Road in Llanelli. He tells Our Pete that he knows his daughter and asks him to take her to a spiritualist church as she will receive a message there that she needs to hear. He tries to show himself more clearly and is putting his hand to his heart and out to Our Pete to show his love and gratitude. Before he leaves, he says, *'This is amazing.'*

Chris

Matthew. He is sucking on his pipe. He tells us to look over Rob's head and identify the colour we can see there. We all agree that it is blue.

Matthew tells Justine *'There are seven energies here for you, your guides and helpers, you have been asking for them. They are blending with you bringing you peace and calm.'* Matthew tells her to look at Rob through her 3rd eye to see the colour of the energy that is being sent to her, via

Rob, by these lovely energies. Matthew is aiding in this. He tells Justine that there are many who want to work with her. He tells her to *'Blend with the light, feel the love.'* Rob feels and sees white energy shooting over and around and through her from head to toe. Matthew tells us we need to be looking, listening, and sensing more. He is delighted to be continuing to work with us.

A new spirit, Chinese male. He has tiny features. He shows us his hands in a gesture of prayer to us all. He has long, dark hair, which is tied back, and he is wearing a green hat. He is also wearing a red robe. He indicates to Mark that he wants to give him healing which Mark accepts. He prays for us and sends us healing. He says that he thinks we are all very special. We thank him for the lovely compliment.

Gethin. He brings through a **Higher Being.** This Being is giving and blending incredible healing energy to us. Both of his hands are bright orange in colour. There are rays of orange light coming out from every fingertip, reaching out into the room, washing over and through us all as he moves Chris's hands. The energy is breathtaking. The lovely Being does this for several minutes then before leaving; he sends a pulse of energy out to us. It was **Amazing!** It really had to be experienced.

SESSION 14
05.10.22

Justine

She is smiling serenely. An older female spirit is coming through. Two shadows can be seen behind her in the box. She is looking directly at Paul and indicates that she knows him. She has a cut or scar to the left side of her mouth. She was asked if she was related to Paul but she shakes her head. She confirms that she had suffered a stroke prior to her passing over.

A new male spirit - He is of Oriental appearance. He has a long moustache, a square jaw, a high forehead and a dimple in his chin. He indicates that he is one of our group guides and works with us all.

Tracey asks if he has come through to give upliftment for Justine as she has been feeling a bit low in mood recently. He nods his head in confirmation. He leaves then to allow the next communicator to come through.

An Indian female spirit comes through next. She has a bindi spot on her forehead. She is one of Theresa's guides. Justine raises her hand, reaching out to Theresa, who then takes her hand. Theresa asks if she has come through tonight to give her reassurances and she confirms this. Theresa says that she experienced a wonderful feeling of calmness and serenity from her. Her name is **Marinda.** She wants Theresa to call on her when she needs reassurance.

Rob

A male spirit is coming through. He is a larger build than Rob and that is seen in the strong overshadowing. He bears a resemblance to the actor John Alderton (Fireman Sam!). He states that he has come through as he just wanted to participate. His surname is Thomas and he lived in Herbert street, Llanelli. His energy is very strong and is overwhelming for Rob. Rob is struggling and it is making him retch. Ange asks the communicator to step back and the communication ended.

Paul

North American native Indian – His name is *White Wolf*. He has a large scar down the left side of his face, pointy ears and long black hair tied back into a ponytail. He has a very powerful energy and is chanting prayers and a blessing on us. He tells us that although he has not been through before, he has been working with us as a group for a long time as part of our learning and development. He reminds us to look with our 3rd eye, to see more than the naked human eye can see. He tells us he is bringing spirituality from the higher levels to us. Before he leaves he says, *'Be blessed.'*

Albert. He tells us that *White Wolf* is **ALL THINGS POWERFUL** and he is known in the spirit world as **'THE CONDUCTOR.'** He says that White Wolf is always present with us and we will continue to see many more guides, helpers and higher energies. White Wolf is also Ange's main guide. Albert confirms that Theresa's guide Marinda came through Justine for her. Albert tells us that as a group we are going from strength to strength. He goes on to say that trials and tribulations are a part of life, but we will stay together as a group. He reminds us that there are many souls that work with us from the spirit side who are also a part of our group. He says, **'Cast doubt aside, when you need us call upon us. No question goes unanswered and nothing goes unnoticed.'**

Albert reminds Ange to hold the golden ticket night very soon. He stresses that, *'There is a need for the public to see this. Whoever the ticket holders are, they must be 100% knowledgeable about what is going on in the trance sessions so that it's not a shock to them.'* He goes onto say, *'Spirit will help you decide who to choose to come.'*

Beth asks about someone close to her who has recently passed over. She wants to know if she has been received. Albert reassures Beth that she has indeed been received and that she didn't hesitate to cross over. Beth asks that because her friend died suddenly, was there anything that she wanted to say to her? Albert says that she will come through when she has found her feet, but reassures Beth by saying, *'She is fine.'*

Ange asks could people have their pets reside with them in the spirit world? Albert replies, *'Yes, they are often the first souls to greet you when you cross over.'* He reassures

Ange that Nancy Boy (her cat) is OK but they call him Puss over there!

Albert assures us that he is going to bring through our family members, friends, guides and helpers in due course.

Colin. He is trying to come through but there are energies pushing in as they are all keen to come through. He is looking to the side of the box and telling them off. He says, *'You can't all come in at the same time.'* He gives up and leaves to allow other communicators to come through.

A new spirit – A lovely gentleman called *Grayston*. He tells us that he was born in Canterbury, England in 1809 and passed away in 1907 aged 98. He had been a gamekeeper on a private estate in Windsor (not the royal estate) then had moved to Shropshire in his later life. The family that he worked for were called the Buckinghams. He says that he had 15 hands (men) working under him, gamekeepers and groundsmen. He had never married as he was entrusted to the Buckingham family. He tells us that he was an educator – his men learnt their trades from him. He says that he has no desire to reincarnate. He explains that we are masters of our own destiny, we have free will, we don't have to come back if we don't want to. However, some souls are pushed to reincarnate straight away, these souls are people that have committed bad crimes when on the earth-plane such as sex offenders and murderers as they must pay their Karmic debt.

He goes on to say that he is a man of leisure in the spirit world, he has his own estate and has used his imagination to create it. He has a large lake with many beautiful fish, Labradors and pointers, pheasants and peacocks. He says, *'Some newly passed spirits have houses presented to them, but you can create your own.'* Grayston tells us that he socialises a lot over there. He explains that on the earth-plane he and his men (hands) had lived full lives serving others, but in the spirit world, *'people who have lived poor lives on the earth plane often have affluent lives in the spirit world and vice versa. It teaches people to be careful how to treat others.'*

Ange asks that if people are very materialistic in this world, do they expect to have the same in the spirit world? Grayston replies, *'The wealth rug is pulled out from under their feet, roles are reversed, teachings are always ongoing.'*

He is delighted to have been given the opportunity to come through as he had not thought that it would be possible.

Colin returns – he says, *'Not staying long, there are loads waiting.'* He jokes, *'Grayston went on and on, he's a bit twp* (this is a Welsh word for being mentally slow), *he was pulled back by the Shepherd's Crook. Mam is making vegetable soup today so I'm off for some of that!'* He tells Theresa off for calling him Col! He jokes to Rob *'Oh you're here again, I thought you'd gone off with the copper!'* He tells us all to **'Keep it going.'** It's always lovely to speak with Colin because he always makes us laugh and that raises the vibrations. He says things which are a bit near the knuckle sometimes but it is said in good humour and taken in good humour. Albert stands close by, armed and ready with the Shepherd's Crook!

A new male spirit comes through. His name is **Raphael.** He greets us, *'Good evening, I lived in Mykonos in Greece. I have been brought forth to tell you of good things to come for the group. You* (group) **will combine your energies with each other to demonstrate to others that life is eternal.'** He

stresses that WE MUST give demonstrations of such. He says, *'Ange will take control of it, you will all have a part to play, step up to the mark, it is time to up the ante.'*

We all laughed nervously but he goes on to say that he will come to us in our sleep state along with other guides to impart knowledge and support. He tells Rob that he must use his knowledge and experience to help us develop as Rob is a highly experienced and knowledgeable medium. Raphael reiterates that, *'The time has come for your teacher to push you.'* He will stand by us to take our nerves away. **He advises, *'Use your spiritual brain, not your physical brain, we will come. Meditate – switch off and we will come. This is a classroom for proactiveness, do not become stagnant.'*** He will be watching us and encouraging us every step of the way.

A new male energy briefly comes through – he has not been through before. He is very harshly spoken, demanding us to **'ask the question'.** We were all confused and didn't ask anything so he left.

Robert Emmanuelle. He quickly comes through after the last communicator. He *says, 'You must learn to recognise when a spirit is brought through to answer a question that you have asked.'* In this case the male spirit that had just demanded that we ask him a question was classed as an 'unfiltered energy' who was willing to answer questions about what is currently happening in the world today. That was a lesson for us to learn. Robert informs us that, *'The suffering in the world is going to get worse before it gets better, there will be an uprising that will reverberate across the world, there is a sleight of hand at play, not all is as it seems.'*

Albert returns – he says that we have been taught a few lessons tonight. He had selected a few guests to come through but we were concentrating too much on the visual (the overshadowing and colours) and not listening attentively to the vocal communications. He goes on to tell Ange that we need to be pushed, to make this group worth something. Raphael is an energy provider and works with us spirit side, Albert is more of a caretaker. He *says,* **'Heed the words of his learned friends, when you meditate ask Raphael to draw**

close. It is not hard to reach spirit, spirit will always reach you.'

Before he leaves Albert gives us each a piece of advice:

To Justine – *'You need to let go'*, she asks him how, he replies, *'Think of me and I will come to you.'*

To Gemma – *'See the career that you are destined to do.'*

To Theresa – *'Stop carrying everyone else's luggage, take it off!'*

To Rob – *'Keep your views under your tongue sometimes.'*

To Mark – *'Prepare for your spiritual awakening again, you have self-healed.'*

To Our Pete – *'Confidence must be put in place, you are the best healer in the group. You are a passionate healer, you have an energy above energies.'*

To Beth – *'Stop worrying about things that you cannot control.'*

To Tracey – *'Make the decision, in regard to the people you thought would mock you, just remember that you are the swan among the ducks.'*

To the group – ***'Always be careful of the lone wolf crossing the field, you are a flock. Raphael is from the highest realms. He is very powerful and intellectual and is held in the highest regard in the spirit world. Prepare for the golden ticket evening!'***

SESSION 15
09.11.22

Justine

She is smiling. There is a male energy coming through. When Chris moved seat, her head turned to watch him walk past. When the communicator was asked if he knew Chris he indicates that he does. He is wearing glasses, has grey hair and a full face. Chris is unable to recognise this gentleman, so he leaves.

A lady comes through, she has curly black hair and is looking at Theresa. Her name is Jan, she was Theresa's best friend. Theresa holds her hand and is very emotional but delighted that Jan had come through.

Chris

A male spirit comes through. His name is **Huw Morris.** He had worked in Cynheidre colliery. He passed away in 1996. He was diabetic and had a massive stroke prior to passing over. He lived in Tunbridge Wells and had been part of the chamber of commerce. He was married to Gwyneth and has a daughter Rebecca. She has children in school, and he says that he is sorry that he couldn't help her as he would have liked to. He has been waiting a long time to have the opportunity to come through and says, *'It is fantastic to come through at last.'* We invite him to come through again when he gets the opportunity.

Matthew. A new spirit also called Matthew is coming through on behalf of our regular communicator Matthew. He tells us that his name is *'Matthew the 3rd.'* He is an educator for us and works with our Matthew. He tells us that he is passing energy to his left side, linking all of us together to form a circle of energy. He tells us that our group has been years in the making. He has huge hands which are directing the energy. He informs us that we will be working on the element of smell tonight and instructs us to imagine that there are sinks in front of us and we must wash our hands in the water and tell him what we could smell. The general agreement was that there was a smell of citrus. He says that they are going to bring us extremely powerful development exercises. They will *'show us, tell us, evidence us.'* He also says that they *'will repay us in no ways that we can imagine, to enhance, and further our spiritual development.'*

He tells us that we each have 3 guides behind us and encourages us to become aware of their presence. With the assistance of other guides and helpers we will experience Out of Body experiences. They will allow us to transcend into the spirit world. We all feel a drop in the temperature and are told that these energies around us are our friends. They promise to show us the journey that we will make on our return to the spirit world. He urges us to *'Be Open and Trust.'* He says that we will be able to recognise early signs of illness in a person and will be able to intervene and support. He says, *'There are great, great things to come.'* He tells us that we are going to transcend but in return we must give them the 'Green light' to do so. He then shows himself more clearly to us – he appears young but strong and powerful, very intense. He looks like a warrior.

Paul

White Wolf comes through. He tells us that as well as being Ange's main guide he is also a guide of the group. He is a Native American Indian Chief. He tells Ange that Blue Feather and Chockday are still present with her, these are her other Native American Indian guides. He advises us *'While the moon is full, absorb its power.'*

Albert comes through as he wants to tell us about ***White Wolf:*** He says, *'**What a remarkable gentleman. White Wolf is one of the highest guides from the highest spiritual realms.**'*

Albert plays a game with us then, telling us to count the birds in the trees and tell him how many there were. He was impressing the number he was thinking of into our minds. It was a test to see if we could pick up on his thought process, it was good fun. He says that he has been teaching lots of new students, new teachers and spirits who want to work with us. He reminds us that we must give them our voices to interact with them.

A new spirit – ***Kenneth Smith***. He tells us that Albert had instructed him to show us something and we had to describe what we could see. We can see that he is wearing a shirt, waistcoat, smoking jacket, and a cravat. He has a pocket watch and his glasses are perched on the end of his nose. He is holding a walking stick in his left hand which has a silver top to it. He says he was born in Kent in 1835 and died in 1906 at 71 years of age. He had also lived in Oxford but then moved to London where he tells us he became *'part of the scene,'* enjoying the company of male friends. He loved parties and would often gatecrash them and was very partial to a brandy or two! He says that he had been a bit of a character and had even bent the law on occasions. He tells us that he had a doctorate in mathematics and his profession as an accountant had been a profitable one! He jokes that he couldn't say any more as, *'The fuzz are in the room,'* meaning Chris who is a policeman.

Ange asks him to describe his experience of passing over to the spirit world. He says, *'I did not believe in the existence of the afterlife when I was on the earth-plane, so it was quite a shock when I died. I was sitting in a chair in the club when I experienced a pain in my chest and the next thing I knew I was sitting next to my body. There were lots of people running around me in absolute panic! I saw a beautiful light and was drawn into it.'* Ange asks him if he would like to reincarnate. He *replies, 'I would like to at some time, but the time is not right yet. I still have lessons that I need to learn here in the spirit world.'*

We begin to see many different people coming through in quick succession, this is to train our vision (clairvoyance). A powerful spirit comes through briefly, his hands glowing luminous orange. He is laughing and says, *'You are my people.'* Then he sternly tells us off, saying, *'You must make the most of opportunities to ask questions and yet you sit here in silence.'*

We had forgotten to ask questions as the spirits were frequently changing. Another new spirit quickly comes through telling us that he is from Bristol, and he had worked on the steam engines, shovelling coal. He was an uneducated man, but he spoke clearly and with good diction. He tells us that every communicator is invited to join 'The Queue.' An old schoolteacher makes a brief appearance, he knows Our Pete as he used to teach him.

Albert returns – He reminds us that we must give the mediums in the box our voices. He believes that we are not quite ready to start seeing family and friends as we are still in awe of spirit. He is disappointed that we are not displaying trust and that the momentum is lost as we have not had a trance session for a long time, it is too long away. He advises us that we MUST HAVE MORE REGULAR TRANCE SESSIONS TO REBUILD THE MOMENTUM. We give our word that we will work harder.

SESSION 16
30.11.22

Justine

A new female spirit, looks angelic and very serene. She has red hair and unkempt teeth and looks like a gypsy. She indicates that she has a good sense of humour and she's smiling broadly at us. The communicators continue to stretch our clairvoyance skills. She appears to be looking at Rob and winking at him, drawing attention to her eyes. We realise that she is indicating she is blind.

A new female spirit – she has a fuller face and a wide nose, which is wrinkled and weathered looking. She is wearing a cape with a hood. Tracey says that she had an image of a horse and cart that this lady would use to take produce to market. She also says that she saw that she would have kept chickens and lived on a farm.

Solomon. He is Angela's Greek guide, he is smiling and looking at Ange but then becomes emotional. Ange felt a touch on her face. He doesn't stay to talk this time.

Paul

New male spirit - Strong, powerful energy, he is a strong character and is highly respected. He is a warrior. He appears to be wearing furs around his upper body. He tells us that his name is *Sia* (Sha). He has just come through to say to us, **'In regard to war, when knowledge prevails there is no need to fight.'**

Albert **comes through** - Justine asks what lessons does Albert teach in his classroom? He replies, *'I teach new arrivals to overcome any anxiety or confusion that they may be experiencing due to their passing. We teach them learnings of love, but also show them the mistakes that they made in their last life on the earth-plane. Many souls achieve all of the objectives/tasks they agreed to meet whilst on the earth-plane, but many do not.'*

Albert goes on to say that we (group)) are all achieving our objectives. *'Once you have experienced and learnt from an objective/task you never ever have to repeat that lesson. Some humans on the earth-plane ignore these opportunities and so don't learn the lessons they need to learn. And so, when opportunities arise grab them with both hands, your guides and helpers will support you – after all, they put those opportunities there for you to recognise and act upon! Reincarnation is a choice, however if you don't tick all of your learning boxes on the earth-plane and then choose to stay in the spirit world, you will be given even more boxes to tick in the spirit world. Learning boxes exist on both sides.'* Justine asks if beings from the higher realms teach in Alberts class and he confirms that they do.

The subject of suicide is touched on again. Albert says, *'When one takes their own life they are in a very difficult position. Their guides try everything they can but one hopes that people around that soul will help as much as possible to prevent that person from taking their own life. To try to help, when you meditate call in loved ones – they are with you and love to be called and to help. When life ends suddenly, the teachings have not been completed. Those souls are given the option to reincarnate soon after. Suicide is NOT a sin.'* He reminds us to **'SPREAD THE WORDS OF LOVE AND FORGIVENESS.'**

Ange asks what happens if a person is suffering chronic pain and takes their own life. Albert says, *'No one wants pain and suffering – taking one's own life is not frowned upon. The thought process becomes all encompassing.'* He goes on to say that we have all had an experience of taking our own lives in a past incarnation. He explains that we must experience everything to be able to share that wisdom and knowledge.

Beth asks, 'When a baby is born, does another person die?' Albert very emphatically says, '*No,* **Our Creator** *would never allow it.* **The Almighty is all things loving.**'

Justine asks if other species on other planets go through similar learning experiences to human beings. Albert replies, *'Whatever life form you are there is always learning to achieve. Human beings are the highest forms of beings.'*

Rob asks about a recurring dream that he has been having, he wants to know why it is happening. Albert tells him that he is *'to learn from the dream but MUST take it as a POSITIVE THING, all dreams, good or bad, are learning opportunities. Some are memories of a past life – experiences that are taken back to a memory state.'*

Tracey explains a dream she had after giving healing to a friend and wants to know what it meant. Albert explains to her that she had been shown two paths for the recipient of the healing to choose from, it is up to the recipient to decide as they have free will. Albert further explains that in our dream-state, relatives and loved ones can step in to help or to offer guidance and support. He goes on to say that this gives us a choice – WE MUST FEEL THE BETTER PATH. He says, 'You must remember to do what feels right to you, listen to your gut instinct.'

Albert advises us that it is beneficial to read books on spirituality and that sounds can help in healing as they resonate, sending the healing vibrations through the physical body. Tuning forks work on this vibration. Think of throwing a pebble into a pond and seeing the ripples extend outwards, it's the same principle. Calm music is best as loud 'bouncing' music has a deeper resonance that doesn't blend well, it can sound frightening eg: the banging of drums can feel 'war-like.' He also advises us to *'BE VOCAL'*- spirit wants to know if they are working effectively. *'DO NOT SIT IN SILENCE!'*

A new male spirit comes through, his name is **Hermando** from Chile. He tells us that he has been asked to give advice on medicine. He says, *'THE ANSWER TO ALL ILLNESS*

IS FOUND IN NATURE.' He says that unfortunately some natural extremely effective plant medicines are abused and have made the use of these natural remedies illegal.

Tracey asks what natural medicines will boost and optimise the immune system? He tells us that a lot of our problems stem from our poor water system. Turmeric and ginger are excellent and hemp oil and fish oil are recommended. He encourages us to EMBRACE GOOD FOOD and put loads of herbs and spices in our cooking. ***'Processed foods are BAD.'***

Colin comes through – He jokes, *'He didn't half go on, mun!'* He tells us that his back is better and someone jokes that he has been having a massage. Colin replies jokingly, *'Up in the Rhondda they weren't really chiropractors!'* He has come to lift the energy. He says, very mysteriously, *'It's all coming to a head, good news is on the way. They are all going to have their heads banged together!'* He makes us laugh by saying, *'The Shepherd's Crook is trying to get me off for what I am saying! Albert has steam coming out of his ears!'* Albert was trying to reign him in but Colin wouldn't have it.

Justine asks if Christmas is celebrated in the spirit world as it is on the earth-plane and Colin says that it is if you want to celebrate it. He is looking forward to it. He has to go then as we are running out of time for this session.

Albert returns then – he says that Colin is the life and soul of the classroom and confirms that we all have something to look forward to. He states, *'Light Always Conquers.'* He reminds us that we must have a POSITIVE MENTAL ATTITUDE and to SPREAD THE WORD. Someone asks, 'When a soul passes over, how long is it before they can communicate with those on the earth-plane?' Albert *replies, 'It could be instantly, depending on their level of awareness of the spirit world when they were on the earth-plane.'* He tells Justine that he works with her in trance and encourages her to call on him. Albert reminds us to ask questions. He says that none will be discounted.

SESSION 17
04.01.23

Mark

A male energy is coming through. He has dark hair, a small moustache, and a scar over his left eye. He looks like Russell Crowe! He appears to be wearing clothing that gives him the appearance of a gladiator. He has a well-built physique. We think that he had been a warrior or soldier. Someone senses a big arena. He tells us that he died age 35. He had been a deep thinker, there is a big book lying open in front of him – he is learned. Perhaps he is a philosopher. He tells us to *'Choose wisely!'*

Justine

There is a female energy coming through. She has been through before. This is Ange's friend Jen. She suffered a massive stroke which had left her disabled. Not long after, she suffered a second stroke which took her over into the spirit world. She had died aged 37. She is getting very emotional. Ange tells her that she thinks of her every day and that she loves her lots. Ange tells her that Mr. Swiston (the cat) is doing very well and is getting on well with Freya (Ange's dog). She also tells her 'The girls are doing fine.' Jen has two daughters and one of then recently had a stillborn baby girl. Jen says that the baby is with her in the spirit world.

A new spirit– a dark-skinned female coming through. The overshadowing is very strong. She is getting emotional as she is coming through. She has a fat face, high cheekbones and wide nostrils. She is a very small built woman and when she smiles, we can see that she does not have any teeth. She looks very happy but doesn't stay much longer.

Paul

Albert says that he hopes we have had a lovely Christmas and New Year. He says, *'Christmas is a season of mixed emotions, good for some but not for others.'* He tells us that Christmas is celebrated in the spirit world by those who wish to celebrate it. We ask if he had celebrated, and he tells us, *'I rested and read a good book on Xmas day.'* He tells us that he had also eaten and drunk in abundance and is very partial to a drop of sherry! He explains that everything looks and tastes better *'over there'*. We can eat and drink in the spirit world if we choose to, but we can only get tipsy!

Albert tells us that some souls, on arrival to the spirit world, need to be taught how to use their imaginations to *'bring things about.'* That is, to manifest what they desire in the spirit world such as food, drink, house, job, lifestyle, etc. Albert teaches this to them in his classroom. He explains, *'desire becomes irrelevant in the spirit world because everything is here – there is no greed, malice, poverty, or inequality. Leaving earthly desires can be difficult for some souls, but when you return to the spirit world you are a Blank Slate'*. This means that all those earthly desires are wiped clean from your mind.

A new male spirit comes through. His name is **BEERACK.** He tells us that he is a Mongolian warrior. He had come through very briefly once before. He says that we are **all** warriors but that *'A war need not be physical. There are many other ways to start, fight and end a war, including chemical, biological and even verbal* (propaganda) *means.'* He explains that the demise of his people came about because they were infiltrated by traitors and he warns us that we walk amongst traitors all the time. He says, *'The powerful don't recognise how powerful they are – they just want more and more all the time because they are greedy.'* He informs us that currently in our world there is a period of calm happening before the storm. *'Greed causes needless war and needless death. War is conflict between good and evil.'*

He is asked to explain why certain people are given the power that they have. He replies, *'They are influenced by negativity, greed and hatred.'* He reassures us by saying *'slowly the light will TURN ON for us* (The majority of human beings). *Change will happen in the next few years, but for change to happen you must have the right people in the right places.'* He goes on to say that currently there is a lot of hatred in the world. *'There has to be a balance, but hate is strong now.'*

Albert returns. He states that many truths are about to be revealed about what's currently occurring on the earth-plane but explains that our freedom of speech is restricted by those who do not want this to happen. He tells us that we, the general public in all of the countries the whole world over, must **UN-restrict** ourselves. He tells us to **'SPEAK UP AND**

SPREAD THE WORD.' He explains that we live in fear of reprisals such as losing our professions (Whistleblowing) but we **'Must all stand together, and the light will be turned on.'** He goes on to say that the influx of souls into the spirit world has greatly increased due to wars being fought around the world. He says, *'Uncertainty is the greatest fear in our world. Some people prefer to SLEEP* (ignore what's really happening). *There are many un-awakened souls on the earth-plane because they are scared to see what is really happening. Those that don't want to wake up – won't!'*

Jill asks, 'Do people pass over when they are meant to? Albert replies, *'Yes, it is all written (mapped out on our lifetime path and documented in the Akashic records).'*
Albert then talks about us gaining confidence to work on the rostrum (platform) and giving one-to-one demonstrations. He tells *us, 'you must demonstrate to gain the confidence. Remember, SPIRIT WILL ALWAYS HELP, SPIRIT WILL ALWAYS REACH YOU.'*

Albert reminds Ange that we ALL must be pushed to our limits, and we will be giving a demonstration of mediumship to an audience in the community centre soon. He tells us, *'BE CONFIDENT THAT YOUR GUIDES AND*

HELPERS WILL BE THERE WITH YOU, THEY ALWAYS ARE.'

Albert tells Theresa that healing is *'THE HIGHEST CALLING.'* She must develop new abilities as she is now much more aware. Theresa thanks spirit for this. Albert continues to say that Theresa has incredible gut instinct. She asks about cutting ties with someone close to her and he reassures her that the ties can always be mended, but he advises, *'Cut they should be.'*

Albert tells us that our guides do not bombard us – THEY NURTURE US – they are with us always. He goes on to say that we will all see spirit walking past us in the street, but we will not know it, they walk alongside us – it is up to us to decide 'Is it spirit or human?' He says, *'Lots of spirit people will not show themselves as they were when they died, especially if there were wounds present or ravages of illness and disease etc. They don't like to, and they don't want to upset their loved ones, but they will show themselves as they previously were in life for recognition purposes.'*

Albert reminds us that **CONFIDENCE AND ADRENALIN are the keys to successful development and experiences**, explaining that **'When confidence and**

Adrenalin are mixed your heart-beat rises and this spurs the spirit-being on to communicate.'

Justine asks Albert for his advice and guidance on OUT OF BODY EXPERIENCES. He VERY sternly tells us that we must NEVER attempt to instigate an Out of Body experience ourselves. If we were to do that our guides and helpers CANNOT help us, and we may not be able to return to our bodies (We would then die). He explains that in trance there must be an earthbound communicator present, such as Ange, who is highly experienced and is our earth-side protector, and Albert or our guides and helpers who protect us from spirit-side. It is then done in a controlled way. He explains that without this protection, negative souls may be encountered – they are like chameleons, they can change themselves and promise you anything to get you on their side. He reiterates that, *'it is an EXTREMELY DANGEROUS PRACTICE, DO NOT DO IT. SOME PEOPLE GET STUCK. When it happens naturally such as in sleep-state, it is a healing experience, your guides and helpers will be present. Meditation should not be practiced before sleep as you will leave yourself open. It is extremely important to remember to ask for protection before meditating.'*

Albert tells us before leaving that The HIGHER REALMS will continue to come through – they want to give us their voices – not so much of the overshadowing. He reminds us to ASK QUESTIONS. Albert explains, *'Those on higher levels have a pure heart and a pure mind and are willing to give back to share the knowledge needed to ascend to higher levels. Our guides are chosen for us by the powers above.'*

AS ALBERT LEFT SOME OF US SAW AN ENERGY OVERSHADOW PAUL, THE BEING HAD A LONG PALE BLUE FACE AND PALE BLUE HANDS. THERESA, JUSTINE, ANGE AND OUR PETE SAW IT. IT SHOWED ITSELF FOR ABOUT 30 SECONDS THEN LEFT. IT WAS AMAZING.

SESSION 18
22.02.23

Justine

She is wearing a black bin bag over her clothes as there is no black cape available. A man's face can be seen in the middle of the bag. There is an old woman coming through, leaning to one side. She doesn't have any teeth but is smiling broadly. She communicates that she has been through before but doesn't know any of us. Another lady (looks like Anne Robinson!) briefly comes through, she has short hair and looks very serene.

Paul

There is a blue mist swirling over Paul's head –it is like a vortex. A Native American Indian male comes through, it is **White Eagle**. He has long black hair and is chanting prayers and a blessing. He says, *'Good evening'* and then leaves.

Albert says, *'Its lovely to have The Boy back.'* (Paul has been away for a while). Ange asks Albert if he will be joining with us all on the platform when we give a demonstration of mediumship to the public. He confirms that he will and adds, *'There are a host of people waiting (in the spirit world) to work with us on the platform.'* He compliments us, saying that we are all improving with our mediumship development. He tells us that there is a Being from the higher levels – ***Xii*** – (pronounced as 'she') waiting to communicate with us tonight but first we can ask Albert questions.

Justine asks if our souls are lifted from our bodies before an impact such as a fall from a high place or a plane crash? Albert replies, *'You would know the fear of the impending impact, at this time most people would pray to THE ALMIGHTY, all would know a sense of peace and calm and they will* **SEE THE LIGHT** *just before impact.'* He reminds us that at our hour of need we look to the sky and pray to THE ALMIGHTY. He reminds us, *'Everything, including human souls, has to be regenerated in one way or another, some ways may be cruel, others natural but they are all lessons.'*

Theresa asks about some of her close friends – she says that they are all having issues with their physical health, and it makes her feel helpless, what can she do to help them? Albert replies that at this time in her life she will experience more of this as we are all getting older. He advises her to give them healing and explains that this alone will give them hope. He says, *'Use healing crystals and demonstrate compassion and love.'* Theresa also asks about a friend who is experiencing difficulties getting pregnant. Albert advises, *'Never give up, there are many different ways to bring up children, eg: adoption.'* He explains that *'due to the humanitarian crises in the world today, there are lots of children that need to be taken in.'*

Ange asks about the war in Ukraine. Albert states, *'Heads will be banged together, however there are some countries that are interfering and fuelling the fire.'* He reminds us not to rely on untrue media stories, saying, *'You cannot believe everything they say. They want you to watch and read what they want you to. They want to sell the news, when it comes to PEACE it sells – but who is buying? There is NO DRAMA in PEACE.'* He advises us to ask questions to the higher level Being who is coming to speak to us, saying that this Being has superior knowledge and permission to answer questions that Albert cannot.

Xii comes through. He is a legion ambassador from the higher level. He tells us that he is Chinese and from The Eastern Province. He has been in spirit since 1218. He explains that he was a hunter/gatherer for the families and that he lived with the land. He had 10 children but only 8 survived.

Jill asks for reassurance that the awful things that are happening in the world currently are going to change soon for the better. Xii replies, *'There is a war of minds going on, but look how far things have already come, people are now talking about the GREED in this world.'* But he warns us that *'People walk around pretending it's not happening as they don't want to recognise how they are being controlled.'*

Someone asks, 'Why is our world changing?' (Meaning global warming). Xii replies, *'It is because of human interference, selfishness, and greed. Mother nature has been around forever, the natural disasters that are occurring have been created by human beings and exacerbated by human beings.'* Xii warns us, *'The TRUTH must come out or this will continue to happen.'* He insists that there **MUST be a change of heart and only we can do that by SPREADING THE WORD.** He reassures us by saying that THEY (THE LEGION OF AMBASSADORS), are here to protect us. Before he leaves, he advises us to *'Remember to always think positively. If you think negatively, you will attract bad luck.'*

A new male spirit. His name is **Robert Smith,** he tells us he was born in 1920 and passed back to the spirit world in 2000 aged 80. He was married and his wife is still alive. He lived in Swansea. He is absolutely amazed at being able to come through, saying *'I didn't expect it to be like this, it's like being back in the Con club!'* He jokes, *'Are you the darts team?'* He says that he is lost for words but doesn't stop talking! He tells us that he was waiting in The Queue and thinks he must have walked through the wrong door! Beth recognises the name of the road he lived in, and they have a conversation about the cost of an ice cream in Crescis! Robert jokes that they cost half a pension. He tells us that he worked down the mines all his life.

Ange asks him to tell us about his experience as he passed over to the spirit world. He says, *'I was sitting in my chair at home, when I had a sudden pain in my stomach that went up into my neck, and the next thing I knew I was looking down on myself. My wife had found me there when she returned from the shops. She called our neighbour to come in and help but it was obvious that I 'had gone.' I then went down the garden to my allotment and when I looked back at my house it was a white light. I knew that I was supposed to walk into the light. Mam was there to welcome me into the spirit world.'*

He tells us that his dad had died when he was a little boy – he had died in the mines. He says, *'I had a wonderful reunion with my family in spirit. I was amazed that although I had had the odd ailment whilst on earth, there was no ailment or pain when I went over. It was all gone.'* He tells us that he is living in a replica of his earthly home, even the Con club is there, and he is waiting patiently for his wife to join him in the spirit world – he says that he won't have to wait much longer. He explains that 'they' (spirit) tell them when someone is about to pass over. They did not have any children, but they were very happy.

He says that he found it a very strange experience looking at himself in that chair. He tells us that they (spirit) walk amongst us. *'It runs parallel see – like a mirror image.'* (He is referring to the earth-plane and the spirit world). He reports, *'I did not suffer, and it was very peaceful but an awful shock for my poor wife.'* He advises us that 'over there' we are all equal, some are wiser than others, but we are all equal. He says that he misses his wife very much, but he is always by her side – he hides her glasses – she knows it's him! He tells us that she is the love of his life, and he is excited for her to experience everything wonderful over there. He says, *'I never get bored over here as there is so much to do. We have access to anything that we desire.'*

He says that there is a lovely little building over there – he opened the door of it, and he came through to us. He advises us to *'relate to each other as they do over there, with equality, love and peace.'* He tells us that he can see his future and past lives in the Akashic records if he wants to, but he is not interested in seeing them. *'The Powers That Be are always around, although sometimes they can't be seen.'* They ask him and others if they want to return to the earth plane. He explains that part of us (a facet) always stays in the spirit world, for example his wife may reincarnate (her spirit will) but HIS WIFE facet will remain with him in the spirit world. He says that it is all controlled over there, *'You can't go off the rails – it is impossible.'* Before he leaves, he advises us to *'LIVE YOUR LIVES, LOOK FORWARDS AND ENJOY YOUR LIVES.'*

Albert returns then and also reminds us to *'LIVE LIFE TO THE FULL – HAVE NO REGRETS – DO IT WITH A SMILE ON YOUR FACE.'*

SESSION 19
15.03.23

Chris

Matthew. He is sucking on his pipe, and we can smell the sweet tobacco he prefers to smoke. He starts the conversation by advising us to remember that although our paths are written, nothing is set in concrete as we have free will. He wants to reiterate what Albert had previously said about Out Of Body experiences, reminding us that we **MUST NOT EVER** try to initiate these experiences ourselves as there is no guarantee that we would get back into our bodies safely. Our guides, although always with us, may not necessarily be able to help us to return to our bodies as the decision to do this would have been our own.

There are, however, some people who like to do this. Unfortunately, this can cause negative reactions in this world. He explains, '*At this moment in time in this world there are negative energies blending as never before, these negative energies are using humans to play out their wishes. The earth is going through a time never experienced before. Spirit is here to help you all, guides are communicating with these people who are experimenting with OOB experiences in their relaxed moments, their meditations and dream states, to try and persuade them not to do it.'* He reassures us that *'Good forces are always in play, those who do not conform to their agreed life plan will be dealt with on their return to the spirit world, as will those who engage in negativity. DO NOT WORRY – SPIRIT IS DEALING WITH THEM.'*

Matthew tells Gemma that she lacks confidence. He tells her that she must speak up and say what she is seeing, this will build her confidence and help her in her spiritual development. He reassures her that she is developing well and that her guides are working closely with her and are very proud of her. Matthew leaves then but promises to return before the session ends.

A new male spirit comes through – he smiles, and we can see that he has teeth missing. His tells us his name is Peter Howells. He died in 1978 aged 50. He had lived in Llanelli. He tells us that he is in utter disbelief at being able to come through to speak with us and had been trying to come through for ages. He was in the 'Queue' and was suddenly pulled in to come through. He tells Ange that he has seen her before on the earth plane, but she doesn't recognise him. He says that he is thoroughly enjoying life in the spirit world, he loves fishing and tending to his allotment. On the earth-plane he had been a smoker and had not looked after himself. He had never married and tells us that he had died of *'blood issues'* but didn't give any further details. He leaves then but promises to come through again if he is given the opportunity.

A new male spirit – this is a Higher Being – he has a very strong powerful energy. He is giving us healing and a blessing. Both of his hands appear huge and luminous orange, the energy is pulsating from him. He has the colour turquoise over his thumbs, Gemma sees this and comments on it and he nods his head to confirm that she is correct. He leaves when the blessing and healing are complete.

Matthew returns – again we can smell his sweet tobacco. He tells us that he and his 3 peers are willing to work with us to develop us spiritually, but he doesn't want to step on anyone's toes. He says that if we want to contact him outside of the trance sessions, we should call on him and he will come to us. He wants us to call on him in times when we may not be feeling ourselves, even when driving. He tells us that we can have a conversation with him, he will hear us, and we will hear him speaking to us in our left ear. We will also smell his tobacco. He encourages us to bring questions for him to the trance sessions.

Paul

A new male spirit comes through. He is a *Powerful Higher Being*. **His name is** *Maow* **– he is an ambassador from THE LEGION.** We have previously met one of his Legion, Xii. THEY ARE A LEGION OF AMBASSADORS from the Higher Levels. Maow tells us that tonight we will all be bestowed with healing. We must listen carefully – we have chosen the path we are on, and we will be rewarded as such. He instructs us to stand up (which we did) and he tells us that a member of THE LEGION (an ambassador) is standing behind each of us placing a robe of healing and love around us individually. We have all been appointed one Legion member as a sign of gratitude for what we do, and we can call upon them to walk with us.

Albert comes through and says, *'A humbling start to the evening.'* The Legion that have chosen us are healing and spirit guides, but they are all Ambassadors and want to be known as Ambassadors. When Paul (The Boy) goes into trance, he goes into Albert's classroom in the spirit world. The Ambassadors had scared Paul when he first saw them as they wear hooded robes and he had thought that they may be negative, but they are higher level beings.

Albert states, *'You are starting to relax and see more, and you must have the confidence to step forward and NOT look back. You **must** believe. Tonight, you have seen THE BOSS (MAOW). The robes of protection that The Legion have placed around you are two feet thick. The Legion are so powerful that they can be called upon at any time for their help.'*

Theresa asks Albert about the upcoming platform demonstration that she, Justine and Rob will be doing soon in one of the nearby Spiritualist churches. He advises us that our Legion Ambassadors will be there with us, and we must trust. They will give a calming influence which will feel like a psychedelic experience. He states that stage fright is normal and that will give us the adrenaline to open the 3rd eye – that is a good thing. He reassures us that Spirit would not put us on the platform if we were not ready – we must do it. Albert will also be there with us.

Some members of our group are training to be spiritual and Reiki healers and tarot card readers. Ange advises that when we are qualified in these abilities, we should charge the client for that service. What we charge is our decision. Albert says that making a living out of demonstrating mediumship is perfectly fine. This can be done in many other ways too, for example working on the platform in Spiritualist churches or centres, one-to-one readings, psychometry etc. He reminds us that *'you are all learning from the ground up'* (which is the best way).

He tells Theresa that she is *'At the top of the mountain in her development'* but that we all continue to learn. Albert tells us that spirit has pulled The Boy to one-side tonight and calmed him as his confidence had been dipping, but now his confidence is sky high. Albert says that he was in the car with Paul and Rob on the way down to group tonight and was listening to their conversation. He says that Paul's wife has pushed him to return to our group because they have been pushing her to get him to return!

Cornelius Chambers – He has white hair and a chin like Bruce Forsythe! We can see a long scar from chin to cheek. He tells us that he was famous in his own right as a journalist for the Times newspaper in London. He is quite posh! Ange asks him what he thinks about modern day journalism. He replies that he is mortified by it but acknowledges that stories must sell. He explains that *'some stories are pure fantasy but if they don't report on these things, they don't get paid. Conspiracies and rumours are often started by journalists.'*

He tells us that we have to see it from all angles – *'The truth must be known but what is the truth? The truth is there, it will come out by natural leakage.'* He goes on to say that some people don't want to see the truth for their own reasons. He advises us not to waste time on what-ifs, but to enjoy life. He draws an imaginary timeline from Beginning to End and puts ENJOY in the middle. He says, *'Life in general is for living, what is a good life? It is the one that there are no regrets at the end.'*

Albert returns – he advises us to take the advice and information given by the spirits who have made the effort to come through tonight. Make sure we take Cornelius's advice as it applies to our own lives. He says, *'PLEASE TAKE COMFORT KNOWING THE LEGION HAVE BEEN BLESSED UPON US.'* It is the highest honour that Albert can think of.

SESSION 20
29.03.23

Justine

A new male spirit – Justine's face has changed and her head is being pulled back, the spirit has a full face and a receding hair line. He indicates that he had played rugby with Paul a long time ago. He has been in spirit for a long time. He was quite young when he passed back into the spirit world. We could see that he had a cauliflower ear from playing rugby. He is turning his head to show his ear. Rob says that he got the name Richard and feels that he and Paul may have played for the same rugby club together, but Paul is unsure.

A new female spirit – she appears aged between 40-50. She confirms, when asked if she had abused alcohol, and this had taken her back to the spirit world. Paul states that he can taste and smell the alcohol. She looks at Rob when he asked if she was a relative of his and nods her head to confirm that she is a relative to Robs mother's side of the family. She has passed over in the last two years. She looks very emotional.

Rob says that he would convey the message to his mum and to her girls and she gave him a delighted big smile.

A new female spirit – she looks unsure about coming through and appears to be seeking reassurance. Her hair is in a short bob. Beth asks her if she knows Beth and she nods her head to confirm this. Beth feels goosebumps, she thinks it is her Aunt Mayer. Beth invites her to come through to her in her dream-state, she nods in agreement.

Paul

A Native American Indian comes through chanting and beating time with his foot. He is a very strong, powerful male energy, it is probably *White Eagle.* He gives us a blessing and then leaves.

Albert. We see that he is wearing a brown tweed suit with a green/gold coloured tie. His white shirt is pristine. PR tells Albert that it's nice to speak to him again as it had been a long time since PR sat in trance. Albert welcomes him and acknowledges that it has indeed been a long time. Albert tells us that there is much change happening in our world. He reassures us by saying, *'There are uprisings occurring now across the world.'* He advises us to *'KEEP THE VIBRATION HIGH'*.

Albert reminds us that Jill had spoken in church about the spread of negativity in the world, and Albert confirms this by describing it as a rapidly spreading cancer for which there is no cure. Justine asks if faith and trust in The Almighty and the spirit world and the spread of positivity will be a cure. Albert agrees that these beliefs are essential but points out that not everyone has faith and trust in positivity, with the media ramming negativity down our throats.

He says, *'Certain groups of people such as the travellers are vilified by jealous people because they do not pay any tax and are free. They also have opinions and are not afraid to voice them. Most travellers are free souls who are targeted by those who do not wish to hear their opinions or do not want others to hear them. There are some travellers who are villainous, but most are very spiritual and community minded, whereas your communities just take.'*

Rob asks a question on Paul's behalf. He says, 'Paul has put something out there (a suggestion) – will it happen?'

Albert replies, *'Yes, it will benefit him and those around him. We* (Spirit) *will do our utmost to make it happen.'* He left it at that.

Justine asks if Angels, Guardian Angels, and Archangels have ever walked on the earth-plane and if they can take the form of an animal such as a dog. Albert replies that they would never take the form of an animal but says, *'Animals are in this world to teach us unconditional love and kindness, they are brought to us for comfort. Although animals are clever, they can only teach us love.'*

Beth asks, 'Why do people fight because of religion?' Albert is very emphatic in his answer: *'Ignorance, pride, and belief that THEY are right. After debate comes violence. Religion is often used as an excuse to start a war. Propaganda is very much involved in religious hatred. However, be mindful that when such souls pass to the spirit-world they are reminded that we are all equal –* **we are all ONE.***'*

PR asks Albert if his father is with his mother in the spirit world. Albert assures him that they are together, joking that they still argue between themselves and that they walk amongst him and his family. He tells PR that they are there to guide and help him, but he must give them freedom to enjoy themselves.

Albert sees this as a good time to advise us of the importance of being organised whilst on the earth plane in preparation for our passing over, as this preparation will relieve a lot of stress and trouble for those left behind, for example, getting paperwork in order.

Beth recounts a dream that she and both of her sisters experienced on the same night. They had all dreamt that their relatives were gathered in a place except for one. Albert tells her that that person is still on the earth plane but would have been invited to attend this gathering in his dream-state. He reminds her that because of free-will, he may have declined to attend. He tells Beth that her dad is very much around her and reminds us that *'dreams can be representative of the past, present and future.'*

Justine asks about a recurring nightmare that she regularly experiences and has done for as long as she can remember. The dream is of huge grey waves on a stormy sea, coming towards her, threatening to drown her and her loved ones. She explains that as well as seeing these waves she hears and feels them crashing against the cliff edge that she is standing on. Albert tells her that spirit is showing her how to stop these waves and that they have been doing this since she was a little girl. He tells her that she MUST stand up to them.

Ange asks Albert if premonitions are at a frequency that only some can experience. He replies, *'When in a state of mind-rest, they will appear. You see more than most because of your ability and you are the most relaxed. The sleep state is the most important part of your daily lives in which your Guardians and your Legion Ambassadors will come to restore you.*

Rob asks why he often wakes up from his sleep laughing but with no recollection of why. Albert replies that *'Laughter is the best form of healing from the spirit world – they are interacting with you through your sleep-state.'*

PR also asks about premonitions. He explains that he will dream something in the night, and it will appear in the papers the next morning. Albert reassures him by telling him he is sensitive and not to be afraid of this.

Jill asks, 'Why would someone in the spirit world stop communicating with us on the earth plane?' Albert reminds us that our worlds (earth plane and the spirit world) are parallel. He goes on to explain that, *'It is important to remember that those in the spirit world, including guides, are ALL PEOPLE. They want to rest and get on with other things, but they WILL return to communicate. NO communicator will EVER DROP OUT. They will be there at your side.'*

Albert promises us that he is going to tap into our sleep-states to communicate with us individually. He says he will appear *'when the time is right.'* He goes on to say that the more we sit in trance, the more they will experiment with us to heighten our awareness. He mentions that there is still some fear and trepidation in the group. He tells Justine that she would be very alarmed if he just appeared in her lounge. He says that before he comes through to us individually, he will send the scent of a homemade lozenge as a precursor to his appearance. He will simply stand and give a nod. He reminds us to visualise energy coming from spirit into the tops of our heads through our bodies and out through our hands directed towards the box. This will increase and heighten the vibration.

Colin. He says, *'Well it's been a while!'* He is talking slowly as the energies are a bit low but insists that he hasn't been drinking! He tells us he has been in his greenhouse tending to his tomatoes – *'No bugs on my tomatoes!'* he says proudly. He tells us that he is going to get new teeth as he has got his eye on a bird! He's bored with doing up his car now.

Tracey asks him if his back is still giving him trouble as he often complains that his back is hurting (although he acknowledges that he could easily heal it himself!) Tracey invites him to come to her for healing, to which he replies jokingly, *'It's not my back that needs healing!'* Albert is at the side of him with his Shepherd's Crook ready to pull him away if he goes too far. He jokingly calls Tracey a *'herbal drug dealer!'* as she always offers advice for ailments that can be found in nature (as can everything.)

He acknowledges that Rob, Theresa, and Justine will soon be giving a demonstration of mediumship on the platform in a spiritualist church. He respectfully acknowledges Our Pete, saying, *'There is no one more spiritual than him, he knows all the churches and goes to them all – fair play. Nice to see PR again.'* He reminds us though that if there is an element of doubt or fear they can't come through.

Colin tells us that he is a proper Rhondda boy, saying, *'it was my boyish charm and poetry that got all the girls – oh – and my giro!'* PR asks Colin if he knows his uncle who is in the spirit world - Joe Stark. Colin replies, *'I'll look him up in the yellow pages now!'* We all laugh at his sarcasm. Ange calls him 'Col' and he tells her off for being too familiar! He informs us that 'physicality' does not stop over there. Ange says that it's called merging, but he says that he doesn't call it that! *'Oh, look out, there's Albert with the Shepherd's Crook!'*

Albert returns – Ange mentions that in a few weeks we will have our first Golden Ticket night and asks how many should be permitted to attend. He says, *'You must decide that but choose wisely, people who are invited MUST believe 100% that the afterlife exists. They will then go home excited by what they have seen and heard and will* **SPREAD THE WORD***. There are 1,000's of communicators waiting to come through.'*

Ange asks if Albert works with any other spiritual groups like ours. He replies that he only works with our group, he has never been part of any other group and he says that he doesn't want to work with any other group. Rob explains that he would like to bring himself in trance to the Sunday services, Albert is encouraging, telling Rob that he almost steps out already – he's nearly there and that Rob's control is PHENOMENAL but his 3rd eye is preventing the step out. His guides will step in front of him.

Albert reminds us to prepare as many questions as we can think of for the trance sessions, saying, *'There are millions of questions that can be answered. It's an opportunity for learning and expanding your knowledge.'* Before he goes Albert reminds us **'DISCIPLINE – *Say what you see.'***

SESSION 21
17.05.23

Justine

An older lady comes through, strong overshadowing. She has a full face, well defined cheekbones and prominent teeth. Gemma recognises her as her grandmother.

A new female spirit – Her name is Dionne and she knows Paul. Paul says that he can see her and she becomes very emotional. Her daughter had given birth this past week and she wants to let her know that she was there with her for the birth. Paul says he will let her daughter know.

Chris

A new male spirit. He has a strong German accent. He tells us that he *'Comes In Peace.'* His name is **Lukas Andrez.** He was a soldier in the first world war and he is showing us some of the injuries he had sustained. He was captured by the British and was a prisoner of war for 6 months but says that he was treated very well. He is trying so hard to speak in English but it is difficult to understand everything he says because of his strong German accent. We encourage him to continue and he thanks us for welcoming him. He hopes to come through again some time.

A new male spirit. David West. He tells us that he was born in 1894 and passed away in 1976 aged 82. He lived near Swansea. He had operated a haulage company which is now run by his nephew. He says that he is shocked by the state of the world as it is now. He is due to reincarnate soon but wants to still be there in the spirit world to welcome his daughter when she passes over. He is having frequent appointments with his guides and helpers in the planning of his new life as he had uncompleted tasks carried over from his earth life that need to be addressed. They are there to guide, support and advise him.

He tells us that he will be reincarnating to Southern Australia as a female. He will be born into a female body on 10.06.26. He explains that we choose our family members depending on the lessons that we will need to learn and the tasks we will have to complete. He describes it as sort of picking from a catalogue but the choices are limited according to those tasks he/she will need to complete. He tells us that he will have 106 tasks to complete but has already chosen how he will pass back into the spirit world at the end of that life. He is looking forward to the challenges of the future.

He had a big family when he was last on the earth-plane and says that he will be born into a big family in Australia. He says that he has been trying to develop for years (earth years) the skills and abilities that he will need to assist him on his return. He is not with his wife in the spirit world but they are still in contact, she has already moved up a level but he says that she is his lifelong soulmate.

Someone asks, how do souls identify each other in the spirit world? He explains that it is through vibration and colour. He warns us that if the tasks we set prior to reincarnating are not met we will bounce right back to the earth-plane. This experience (trance) is aiding his development and skill set as well as ours. He tells us that we are doing a brilliant job and that spirit are very, very proud of us. He tells us that there is a lady called Dilys at the side of him who is chomping at the bit to come through. He leaves then but promises to come through again.

Matthew – he is still having difficulty with his voice. It is very deep and soft and his words sound a bit garbled. It is very difficult to understand everything he is saying. For some reason the energies are not quite blending properly. He says, *'It's a bloody shambles!'* Matthew agrees with David's description of how we choose our families for our next lives on the earth-plane, but wants to clarify that the selection of people to choose is limited as they will all have to fit into the life-plan together. He says, *'The family that David will choose will all have tasks to complete within that family that will match to his tasks and learning requirements. David will experience similar unpleasant learning situations in his new life in Australia that he created and was responsible for in his last life. The number of tasks related to those things that he will need to achieve varies in relation to the severity of the original situation. The purpose of tasks is to learn from them and to give something back out of that learning, perhaps to educate others about it to prevent that negative behaviour occurring amongst others. This will demonstrate to his guides and his leaders that he has wholeheartedly learnt and developed and will significantly reduce the number of his tasks. If you wrong someone, you must realise* *it and try to amend for it and feel that you have then done the right thing, that task would then be completed, and should not be held against you.'*

Matthew advises us to try and identify what our tasks are in this life and to learn from them, but also to endeavour not to pick up new ones! He warns us that we must speak to our guides first before doing this as it could be seen as cheating.

Matthew tells us that we should not think 'why me?' in situations that develop in our lifetimes, for example a serious illness or life-changing accident or other trauma, be it physical, mental or emotional. He says, *'You must overcome these thoughts. Remember, there is no such thing as a tragic passing or passing before your time. It is all planned, it is all written, it is all part of the agreement that you made with your guides prior to returning to the earth-plane. Any feeling that you experience that causes you worry, that creates a feeling of fear, unhappiness or anxiety* (anything other than happiness) – *that feeling is attributed to a task or challenge. Anxiety is just a feeling caused by the human brain which is linked to the task, nothing else. For someone who suffers with permanent anxiety, fear or unhappiness and worry, all of these feelings may be related to one big overall task. In that case, when you overcome these feelings yourselves, you must use your experience and knowledge to help others overcome those emotions by devoting your time to them. This will enable you to absolutely complete your task.'*

He tells Ange that her commitment and dedication to Spirit and to us as a group is helping her to complete one of her tasks. He applauds her for doing so by saying that there are not many people who would do that when they are experiencing the physical pain that she is constantly enduring. Before he leaves he tells us that he has many friends in the spirit world that want to work with us in different ways. He doesn't expand on that though as he is pulled back.

Paul

*A **Native American*** comes through and gives us a blessing. His chanting is soothing and calming but resonates powerfully through all of us and out into the room.

Albert comes through. Gemma asks Albert to give her some information on her last earth-life prior to this. He tells her that she was a female and she was Dutch. Physically, she looked similar to how she looks today. He says that there is a photograph of her in a book where she can be seen standing next to a windmill. He will tell her the name of the book that the photograph is in and she will see it.

Ange also asks him to tell her about one of her past lives. He tells her, *'You were a female goat herder in Switzerland. You had an affinity with dogs and used them to herd your 1,000s of goats. You were a nomad and lived amongst your animals and you made cheese and butter.'*

He tells Theresa that she has waited a long time to retire and now that she has she must take the journey in her stride. *'You will be as busy as ever.'* She replies that she feels the influence from the spirit world is helping her greatly.

Albert reminds us that many months ago our guides introduced us to The Legion. He says, *'At any time you feel down in the dumps or a little neglected, you must call on The Legion and they will be there to help you. They are helping to bring the journey of positivity into your lives. Your guides and the Legion are from different levels. The Legion beings are from a very high level and they are truly respected by your guides.'*

Albert tells Ange that she is going to be busier than ever, teaching an abundance of subjects, for example, Spiritual healing, Reiki, mediumship and tarot. He reminds her that this is her path. She accepts this and is happy to do so. He also reminds all of us to *'never let self-doubt creep into your positivity.'*

Justine tells Albert that she recently saw a gentleman in a restaurant that was wearing a green and gold thread tweed jacket. He had dark but greying curly hair and was wearing a hat that matched his jacket. He instantly reminded her of Albert. He saw her and smiled and nodded to her. This is something Albert had said he would do. Albert acknowledges that it was indeed him and that we all will see him many more times to come. He promises to tip his hat the next time.

Tracey tells him about a gentleman she had seen in the hospital recently who had tipped his hat to her, he acknowledges this too. Chris says that Paul has been feeling unwell and asks if those that work with him in the spirit world also feel that illness. Albert replies that they will not feel the illness but they will 'encourage' Paul to go to the Doctor. They will also send him healing and put protection around him. It is the same for all human beings.

Before he leaves, he tells us that we are being told from *The Highest Realms that WE ALL 'MUST ENJOY THE MOMENT – BEING PRESENT IN THAT TIME AND PLACE, LIVE LIFE TO THE FULL. DEPRESSION AND ANXIETY ARE TOOLS OF NEGATIVITY. ALWAYS TURN A NEGATIVE INTO A POSITIVE. DON'T ALLOW NUGGESTS OF NEGATIVITY TO FESTER. BANISH NEGATIVITY, RUMOUR, DECEIT AND GOSSIP. GOSSIP HAS A PROFOUND EFFECT ON OTHERS.'*

He tells Justine that he has spoken to her guides and they are all in agreement that she should start speaking soon in trance, as she is very frustrated that this has not yet happened despite the overshadowing being so strong. He says, *'You need to be more confident and relax more. It will not be your voice that you will hear and you may jibber jabber but that is perfectly OK.'* He tells us to call for him if we want to see him in our sleep state. He jokes that his arm will be aching from tipping his hat so much! He reminds us to say a little prayer to ask for the higher realms to help us get a good night sleep. Justine jokes that there will be nothing going on in her bedroom and Colin hears that and chuckles, saying he'll be there!

SESSION 22
24.05.23

Justine

A Female spirit – an elderly lady, she has lots of chins, is wearing glasses and has short grey hair. Theresa asks her if her name is Monnie, she indicates that it correct. She is Theresa's aunt. Theresa tells her that she and her family were only talking about her last week and that she misses her laughter. She acknowledges that Theresa's mum is not well at the moment.

Paul

A new male spirit – his name is Chamoon. He is Egyptian. He is chanting a blessing and welcoming us. We can see a ring of jade green around his neck and at the top of his head. He says that he was a manual worker when he was on the earth-plane. He is Chris's permanent guide. He says, *'I have always been with Chris, although Chris has many other guides too and they all play a part. My role in Chris's life has been to bring him strength. Chris has needed strength from an early age. I have met with him several times in his awareness.'* He promises to show himself to Chris soon. He doesn't know how old he was when he passed over but thinks he was between 38-42 years. He tells Chris that his wisdom MUST be shared amongst his children, the youngest has intuition and it will come to him. Chris must talk to him and call on Chamoon when he is in need. He tells him that their love is binding.

Derek Jones. – He has never been through before, we are all trying to guess who he is and he tells us to shut up for a minute! He says that he was 79 when he passed away in 1985. He used to live in Swansea and was in charge of an Allotment Society. He says, *'I had a heart attack just as I was going into my shed on my allotment to make a cup of tea.'* He says that he wants to make a point tonight. He wants to make his presence known, saying that his name has been disparaged. He says, *'For four years on the trot I had prizewinning marrows and carrots. Another allotment member Paul Smith who lives in Swansea (still on the earth plane) is claiming that it was HIM that had them! I want him to know 'I did NOT put slugs in his pots! He is a wicked man, someone in your group will come across this man soon.'*

Tracey tells him that she is from Swansea and he says to her, *'Listen to me now Ginge! You set the record straight! I grew my carrots in peat and soil and that bas***d told everybody that I had horse s**t brought down from Maesteg. I know he nicked it because I knew the farmer and he doesn't. The farmer's name is John Jones. Paul Smith made £16,000 off honey from his bees, but the tax man doesn't know it and if I was still alive he'd have a letter under the door. He's a wicked man.'*

Tracey says that karma will get him and he replies, *'It already has! He came 2nd in the Gower show with his radishes! Mark Evans beat him and he couldn't grow s**t! Mark had help from me because he had my horse s**t! You've only got to throw a seed in it and run like f**k! It will be like Jack and the Beansprouts!'*

He apologises for swearing as he is being told off by Albert. He tells us not to rely on the supermarkets for our produce and advises us to *'buy 2 tonne of John Jones's horse s**t and you'll have the best tasting tomatoes you've ever tasted. You taste one of my tomatoes and you'd know it was mine, grown in John Jones's s**t! I had two tonnes delivered just before I died and I hadn't even gone in the box yet when* *they were all like vultures grabbing my s**t. I just can't let it go! Paul Smith is a charlatan!*' He tells us that even though he knows he has to get it off his chest and let it go he can't until the record is set right. He is happy now that he has got his point across. We are all in hysterics!

Albert. Justine asks about the purpose of the journal. How do we spread the word? He replies, *'As your journey continues the journal will grow, and at some stage you will turn it into a book. Justine will have to adlib at some stages to explain things to the readers who know nothing about trance.'* Albert reassures her that everything that we are told can be written.

Tracey asks if the information within the journal can be shared to others who are interested in the spirit world. Albert replies, **'***Yes, as that will help to* **SPREAD THE WORD.***'* Ange states that although there are other books on the market about trance, they are usually one medium and one communicator. This book will be unique in the sense that we have so many characters coming through and 3 mediums in each session. Albert informs us that Patrick (the fishmonger) has transitioned back to our world but he is not at liberty to say where he has reincarnated to, but says that he has gone back to familiar ground. He also tells us that Gethin is on a journey himself. He is spending time with The Elders on the Higher Levels and it is a learning experience for him.

A female spirit – Julie Williams – it is her first time coming through. She tells us that she lived in Hackney and died in 1973. Tracey asks her if she had arthritic hands, she replies no but her hands were vital to her profession. She informs us *'I was a government spy on the switchboard in the telephone exchange during the 2nd world war. I would intercept messages and codes and report back. I would only listen, not speak. I was unmarried as my job was my life. I chose my profession as my life.'* She says, *'When you sign the Official Secrets Act you have to abide by it. I worked as a civilian in the telephone exchange not to arouse suspicion and therefore remained anonymous. I would also intercept messages from those of a villainous nature. They were brought to justice. It still goes on.'*

She says that she is considering reincarnating but is happy where she is at the moment. *'I was on my own when I passed away, but it was a peaceful passing. I was looking at the fire and it became mesmerising, drawing me into it. I became aware of a feeling of incredible warmth around me and saw a beautiful light that drew me to it. At that point I knew I had passed because my aches and pains had all disappeared. The feeling of floating was wonderful. I felt compelled to go towards the light and was greeted by my parents, I had lost touch with them at a very early age because of my choice of profession. I had to cut all ties with my family and friends.'*

She says that although today she would be known as a spy she *'would rather be known as a person of interest.'* She tells us that she has wonderful experiences in the spirit world and is doing things there that she couldn't do in her lifetime on the earth plane. She tells us that she has a message for us all *'The best tools you have are your heart and your stomach, always go with your gut feeling and listen to your heart.'* We thank her for the sacrifices that she made for us all in her life on earth.

Cornelius Chambers – He is sitting with his legs crossed and looking at Chris. He tells us that he wants to be the headliner in the book. He is flirting with Chris and is making us all laugh. Justine asks him if he is going to assist with the writing of the book but he says, *'Proof writing is not my speciality, my dear!'* He tells us that it was very difficult to be himself when on the earth plane as his gay lifestyle was illegal then. He had to learn 'The London Code' and had to be very careful in his private life. He used to be a journalist himself and reminds us that *'newspapers manipulate the mind and corruption rules the world.'*

He informs us that electric cars will quickly become the only transport of the future, that will be happening soon. Cars are going to become so expensive that we won't be able to afford them as the minerals that make the batteries are running out. There will be more public transport and increased use of electric motorbikes and scooters. The very rich will be the only ones driving as only the very rich will be able to afford to do so.

Tracey asks about Global warming, is it really occurring or is it natural evolution speeded up by human interference? He replies, *'How hot has it become? Where is the evidence to show these increases in temperature? Countries around the world are pumping trillions of taxpayers money into climate change but there are millions in the world living in poverty and starving. They should be pumping those trillions into the cost-of- living crises.'*

Unfortunately the trance session then ran out of time. **Albert** returned briefly to say goodbye.

SESSION 23
21.06.23

Justine

Strong overshadowing. ***An older lady*** coming through, she looks like she has been in a fire, there is a burn and a scar under her chin, she turns her head to show us more clearly. She has prominent front teeth. She confirms that she died in an accident and has been in spirit for a long time. Jill feels there is a little boy standing on Justine's left hand side.

Another lady comes through. She has a full face and wide nostrils. She doesn't appear to have any teeth. She is a bigger build but not very tall. This is Gemma's grandmother Annie. She died when Gemma's mum was 14 so Gemma had never known her, but she recognises her from photographs.

Chris

Matthew **comes through.** He has redness around his eyes and he is turning his face for us to see it. His voice still sounds distorted. He is trying to raise the vibrations and sends energy around the group telling us to be sensitive to the back of our necks, starting with Ange and going around. The energy is evident and we can all feel it although it is very subtle. It is a pleasant tingling sensation. He tells us that our guides are also assisting in this.

Matthew tells us that there is an Angel-like figure coming in to the back of the room. He tells us to be open and that we have full protection. We feel a very positive energy coming forward. We close our eyes for 10 seconds as instructed and can feel the energy on the top of our hands, it feels like a weight in each hand but it's a nice feeling. He then tells us to feel the energy work its way up our arms. He is very happy that we can feel this energy and tells us to take this energy into our bodies. He says we are extremely fortunate to be receiving this healing energy, as it is coming from him, his peers, our guides and the Angel-like figure in the room.

The energy appears to pulsate as we embrace it, it is getting stronger and stronger and flooding through our bodies. He says, *'There is more energy in the room at this moment than an atom bomb! Enjoy the moment. There are senior figures from the spirit world behind you, sending love and devotion to your group. I have never experienced so much power before.'* He warns us, *'The technology which is being forced upon you in your modern world can desensitise you, taking you away from your spiritual journey in more ways than one. The technology is aiming to disrupt your thought processes and your connection to your human spirit. There is a significant element of control in your world and sleight of hand, hidden under the guise of things happening and decisions being made for your benefit.'* He encourages us to make our own decisions as far as we can on our individual journeys.

Matthew reminds us that **we are all ONE, all of us on the earth-plane and all those who reside in the spirit world.** The only difference is that we still have our physical bodies to carry us around whereas they are beings of light.

Someone asks if there is a limit to the number of souls in existence. He explains that we are recycled. He says, *'You need to understand that the way you are recycling your goods is like our journey. You are born onto the earth plane and live here a short time, hopefully completing the tasks and learnings you agreed with your guides to undertake prior to returning to the earth-plane, and paying your karmic debts, before returning again to the spirit world. In time, and as your knowledge and experience grows and you have learnt from all of the tasks you have undertaken, both on the earth-plane and in the spirit world, and your karmic debts are paid, you will develop onto the next tier of your journey. At this point you won't ever need to return to the earth plane again. There are many tasks to do and many lessons to learn so reincarnating to the earth-plane happens many times.'*

He goes on to explain, *'When on the earth-plane, individuals can drop back to lower tiers (levels) if they sin and then they would have to return more times to the earth-plane to prove that they have learnt and grown from their mistakes. You can move up and down the tiers quite easily. This does not happen in the spirit world as there are never any sins committed.'* He says, *'When you come back to the spirit world you soon realise that the amount of spiritual beings has never increased or decreased. It remains the same, but what happens is that spirits will move tiers. In my eternity, I have never known there to be any more or any less energies created on our path. All of us are in the same pool together, you are on the earth plane for an agreed period of time and then you will leave and return, leave and return. It is not until you have completed all of your tasks will you be granted on to the next level. On the next level you will also have tasks to complete and when you have done so you will move up to the next level after that and so on. If you don't complete all of your tasks you will remain on that level. It's really simple. You are all here now because of your past lives. I advise you all to do a dedicated meditation on regression and past lives. The second you pass back over into the spirit world you will remember everything, within a millisecond.'* He tells us that we can also go back in time.

Paul

A Japanese spirit comes through quickly. His name is ***Nacorrow.*** He has come to give us all healing. He tells us that he is one of the groups helpers and he joins us on a Thursday evening with Chow Ling to assist us with the healing course some of us are currently undertaking. He has a lot of green energy around him. He says that he worked with medicine when he was on the earth plane. He has worked with other groups but he has now been invited to work with our group.

Albert – greets us with his customary warmth and fondness. Although it was an unplanned trance session from our side it was not short notice for him! He was always aware that it was going to happen. Nothing happens by coincidence or accident.

Ange asks him what he likes to do in his spare time in the spirit world. Albert replies, *'I read a lot and go for long walks, the spirit world is beautiful beyond description in human words. Many spirit people wander the lands for eternity. I travel extensively through thought. As you know, there is no need to sleep in the spirit world, but you can if you want to. I have a lovely log cabin that I retreat to at times.'*

Justine asks him again when she is going to start talking in trance and he tells her, *'It will happen. When you build a snowman you don't put the carrot on first, you build the head, the body and put the hat on etc and the carrot for the nose comes last. The conditions have to be right, too hot it melts, to cold it never forms. It all takes time.'* What he means is that it is still a work in progress for her. She asks him what she needs to do and he replies, *'You do nothing, it will come.'* He tells her that when she is going into the trance state she is blocking herself because she wants it so much, but she can't make it happen. He tells her to remember that this is a joint effort between her and spirit. He reassures her that she is not doing anything wrong and reminds her of how far she has come on her journey.

Justine asks Albert if he can give her information about her last life on the earth plane. He tells her that in 1746 her name was Peter Redmond and that he was a tailor. Born in Illingworth. He was married to a Welsh girl and had a son named Sebastian and a daughter named Bethan. He lived a very happy life. He died at 76 years of age, not long after his wife's passing. He had dark hair, 5'9' tall. We all have many lives and he was not her last life but the one before that.

Ange asks about one of her past lives. Albert tells her that she was born in 1846, into a wealthy family. She lived in a stately home and was a socialite. She never worked. She was married to a Captain Mark Armstrong who unfortunately died in battle. They didn't have any children and she never remarried. She was highly educated and went to Oxford University. Her name was Genevieve Winston. She died age 69 years. There is a picture of her in a book posing with an umbrella.

Cornelius Chambers. He tells us that Albert is a learned and dear friend of his who is held in the highest regard in the spiritual realms. He says that he has been given permission to say what he wants to tonight.

Tracey asks him what he thinks about gender identity. He replies, *'People can be what they want to be, I had a wonderful life but times change.'* She asks if sexual preferences are genetic, he replies mischievously, *'I just like willy!'* Albert is standing nervously to the side with the Shepherd's Crook! *'I still have the desire in the spirit world but I like both men and women. I'm not bisexual – just greedy!'* He explains that this does not however influence his other lives.

He tells us that there are worlds that are far more developed than ours, but also many that are far less developed. He encourages us to not dismiss development and *'yearn to return'* to the earth plane to fulfil strong desires, desires which are not so strong can be fulfilled in the spirit world. Cornelius moves on to discuss the current affairs on the earth-plane before the time is up for the session.

SESSION 24
19.07.23

Justine

An elderly lady is coming through – looking down but with eyes open, no teeth, very old. She is bending right over, shrinking into herself. She has a tiny frame. Her whole body is tight and her neck and hands are very aged. It appears that she had scoliosis at the end of her last earth life. Her face is really small, her nose is very bulbous and her cheekbones and chin are sunken in. She had been a hard working lady during her life and had worked into very old age, she indicates that she had had no choice.

Paul

A new male spirit – his throaty chanting is resonating through our bodies. He appears to be bestowing blessings upon us. He says that his name is ***Keesar*** and he was born in Mongolia. He tells us that he had been a healer when he was on the earth-plane. He says that this is the first time he has been able to come through to us. He is one of Paul's guides – a new one. He tells us to tell Paul that he has a lot of spiritual work ahead of him. He chants loudly again in Mongolian before leaving.

Albert. Theresa asks Albert if he has heard her prayers, he confirms that he has but encourages us all to send our prayers to our own guides first. He states that no prayer goes unanswered. Theresa asks about her mum, giving Albert full permission to tell her the truth. Albert very sensitively tells her that it is not going to be long before her mum passes into the spirit world. He tells her that Theresa's grandmother is standing guard awaiting to welcome her over. Theresa will be there at the time of her passing. He tells her that when the time is right she will run to her mother. Albert advises Theresa to keep speaking to her mum and give her mother a password for mediums to pick up on when she comes to communicate, then Theresa will know that she is safe. He assures Theresa that her mother is never on her own and assures her that everything she is doing for her mum is correct. He tells her to look into her heart for the answers. He will stand with her in each moment that she calls him. Theresa jokes that she wants to thank the Angels for keeping her a parking space every time she visited the hospital, and Albert replies, *'It's not what you know, it's who you know!'*

Justine asks if there is a difference between a dimension and a universe. Albert replies, *'They are one and the same thing. Some are mirror like, that is, they appear the exact same as our universe and then others are completely different. There are many universes.'* He states that he understands that we are curious beings and want a deeper understanding of what is out there.

He confirms that portals exist. They facilitate beings to travel from other dimensions into our world and to subsequently return to their own. Justine asks if worm holes exist in space in which spirit-beings can travel from one dimension to another. Albert explains that these are the portals he is telling us about. He informs us, *'you will see a portal through your third eye.'* He warns us to be very careful about looking too much into these things as human beings, saying *'Curiosity will blow your minds.'* Human beings cannot travel through these portals/wormholes.

Beth asks why she is always scared of the dark. Albert tells her that it is to do with a past life of hers. Her name was Rose and she was a pickpocket. She had lived on the outskirts of Jerusalem and was imprisoned by the Romans when she was aged 13 and put into a dark chasm. There was no natural daylight. She remained in there until she died aged 15. There was no mercy shown for thieves, especially females. Beth says that she has always wanted to go to Jerusalem and Albert tells her that it is her calling to go there. Albert tells her that he will help her, with the assistance of one of her guides, to help her overcome her fear of the dark.

Our Pete tells Albert that he has been reading the bible, and asks if it is true that Jesus Christ is going to return to Jerusalem. Albert replies that *'nothing is impossible'*, and that Our Pete is talking about the Reawakening. He says, *'Our Saviour's son will reappear, he could be in you, it is HIS choosing. It won't be a Biblical event – he will always arise when needed.'*

Ange asks Albert if those in power on the earth plane at this time will achieve a one world order. Albert replies, *'Not in your lifetime.'* He explains that this has been going on for many hundreds of years giving examples of the Romans and the Nazis. Both regimes wanted to be a one world government.

'This is not new as such, you are controlled by corruption and greed. There will be revolt, it is starting as we speak.' He goes on to explain that our guides and those in the higher realms will always put a dampener on 'their' (negative energies) proceedings but warns us that they are a force because they can control everything. He reminds us, *'People believe what they want to believe, and what they hear and see. It is called propaganda'.*

Tracey asks about spiritual ascension. 'On this earth plane we are currently living in a 3D dimension, can we achieve a 5th dimension of spiritual awareness? Do people such as monks live in this 5th dimension enabling them to rise above all earthly desires and temptations, mentally and spiritually?' Albert advises us to ask our native American, Aborigine and Mongolian spirit friends for the answers to that question. But he does say, ' *You have to have the belief. There are places in your world where you can acquire psychedelic agents of a natural kind that will help you achieve this psychedelic experience of going within yourself and stepping out, with natural agents that have an hallucinogenic effect, but your minds are too confused and busy to enable you to let go in its entirety. But it can be done – Dimensions upon Dimensions.'*

Albert states that we have all experienced these states already or we wouldn't be here now, in this group! *'You can reach states of euphoria just by meditating – the art of meditating is an art in itself.'* Albert jokingly scolds Paul, saying, *'One minute he's drifting off in meditation and the next he's wondering how to get a JCB through his house!'* (Paul is a builder and is currently undertaking renovations in his garden.) *'The art of meditation is the best form of healing you can get.'*

Tracey states that she gets to a state of euphoria when she is giving healing. Albert reminds us that it's important to find some quiet space and time to meditate. *'One can achieve anything that one desires.'*

Ange asks if when planning the life you will next live on earth, as we have free will, do people choose to be murdered to have that experience or is it karmic debt? Albert replies that it is karmic debt. He says, *'No one chooses to die. It goes along the lines of having several scenarios to choose from in order to have that experience. They will have wronged in a previous life and must have the lesson to understand where they went wrong. Karmic debt works in various guises. No one chooses to be killed or to kill another person in their life plan, it is all about the teachings and the learnings in life, there is no hatred involved.'*

Theresa asks if you would choose to be a murderer, or is it evil that takes hold? Albert very firmly says, *'That is a side which I do not want to discuss in this group.'* He is reminding us that we *'do not want to venture into the dark. Keep it light'*.

A new male spirit comes through – he is very surprised to see us, and is being very shy and coy. He is shrieking with laughter, making us all laugh a lot as he keeps doing it. He has never been through before. It is obvious that he had learning difficulties in life. His name is **Neil.** He had lived in a home all of his life and his parents had never gone to see him. He was singing over and over again *'Don't you come complaining to me.'* He tells us that the nurse in the home used to sing that to him all of the time. Of course, on returning to the spirit world, that condition had immediately left him and he is perfectly well. Tracey reminds us to be grateful and appreciative of the lives that we have got.

Cornelius Chambers. He says he has *'just dipped in.'* He advises us to awaken our children to what's going on in this world. We discuss this more in depth. Before he leaves he reassures us that there will always be people fighting for truth and justice and not to live life in fear. He reminds us to *'Live for today.'*

Chow Ling comes to give us all healing. We all hold hands, forming a healing circle. We receive healing for the information that Cornelius had just given. Chow Ling knows when to come without being asked.

Albert returns – He says that Cornelius is a lovely man, he has known him for many years but he warns Cornelius to be careful of what he says, as there are some of us in the group who don't want to know too much of what is going on in the world as it causes us worry. Albert says that although they in spirit can see further ahead, they are unable to interfere because of free will, but he does say that they will put a **FEELING** into our solar plexus chakra, so to listen to that, our gut feelings, as it is these feelings that are telling the truth.

Before he leaves, Albert says, ***'Don't let these wonderful evenings end. You all need to give your lives to others. Talk to others, give your life stories. The spirit world needs you to speak up on our behalf.'*** He tells us that he was so proud when he stood on the platform with Theresa, Rob and Justine in the demonstration of mediumship they had taking part in recently, as he knew it was for the benefit of others. He reminds us that what is so important, is how a message is received. *'Your experience, your life stories, people relate to them. That love is portrayed to the audience when you give them a message. It's not about self-reward.'* He tells us to relax and enjoy the experiences. *'Keep the questions coming.'*

SESSION 25
23.08.23

Paul

*A **strong male energy*** comes through, he is chanting prayers and blessings upon us. He is helping to lift the energies as they are a bit low tonight as a lot of the group members have had a difficult week. The sound resonates throughout our bodies through our chakras. It is very loud and powerful.

Albert. Albert tells us that the last communicator giving the healing is one of our group guides. His name is ***Xian Xii.*** He is a Tibetan monk. He has been with our group since its inception. He asks how the information that we give out to the general public is received. We are able to tell him that it is on the whole, very well received. Most people are very interested and want to know more, some are sceptical but it is rare to find anyone who completely disbelieves in the existence of the spirit world and the after-life. He says encouragingly, *'When you work spiritually you may be rewarded for such.'* This may even be in ascending to another level.

Theresa speaks to Albert about the awful times she has experienced recently, losing three members of her family in quick succession, one of them being her mum. She tells him that she felt lost and abandoned by spirit and apologises for swearing at him! He tells her not to worry and says, *'When grieving, the heart and the mind combine to produce strong thoughts and emotions not normally experienced or spoken, some meant, some not meant.'* He reassures Theresa by saying *'Your mum has been received in the spirit world and despite her mobility issues she had run here!'* He jokes that she was probably running from Theresa!

He reassures her by telling her that her mum was with spirit before her physical body died. *'Put all of your fears and memories of her passing to one side and let them go, looking back will get you nowhere. Move forward, forget about what happened, for your mum's sake. She is at peace now. Your brother came to meet her and she fell into his arms, the love was bursting from him.'*

He mentions a little dog being very significant to someone over there. He tells Theresa, *'Don't ever doubt yourself and your spirituality, they are all tests. Your world is so cruel. That word cruelty has many definitions, emotional and physical damage, you cannot be responsible for grief. Mam is at peace, free from illness and pain. There is a whole network of people there welcoming her in. She is aware that you are experiencing feelings of guilt and she wants you to stop torturing yourself as you have nothing to feel guilty about – far from it.'*

A new male spirit – He has not been through before. Ange comments that he looks like Telly Savalas ('who loves ya baby!') He has a lovely benign smile. His name is Brigadier John Samuel. He was born in 1831 in Basingstoke, England and died in 1893. He was a Brigadier in the Royal Brigade, the Queens service, and was stationed in India for much of his life. He had eventually returned to England and tells us that he died of natural causes, a general deterioration in his health and mobility due to the natural ageing process.

He says, *'Just before I passed over, I remember that I was laying in a hospital bed. I just lifted out of my body, it was very peaceful and I knew where to go and that it was important that I knew that. I had been a bit sceptical about being able to return to the earth plane through the medium of trance but I was waiting in the queue and suddenly it just happened. I am absolutely amazed and can't believe my eyes. It is extraordinary, unlike anything I have ever seen.'*

He can't quite make us out or who we are and wonders why we are here. He says that he FEELS (senses) us. Visually we are just shapes to him. He reminds us that it is a two way lesson. Whilst we in group are developing to communicate with the spirit world, likewise the spirit world are learning to communicate with us on the earth plane. He explains that he felt *'like the chosen one'* when he was picked out of the queue. He describes the queue as being *'comprised of all colours, creeds, races, religions etc and is many people wide and further than the eyes can see.'* He admits that he was very sceptical about the existence of the afterlife whilst he was on earth, so it was a bit of a shock when he passed over to see that it is true.

Colin. We tell him we've missed him as it's been a long time since he joined us last. He is asked if he works with any other trance groups but he says that he only works with our group. He jokes that he wouldn't work with any other group as *'they may send me back to the valleys and I owe Dai the Milkman £40.00!'* He is full of jokes as usual and is making us all laugh. He says that he used to love going on holiday to Trecco Bay in Porthcawl. Born in 1956, he was 6'4' His full name is Colin Jones – *'not the boxer!'* His father's name was Aneurin. Aneurin used to work in the Big Pit. His mother's name was Dorothy. Colin worked as a mechanic but did go into the pit on occasions but did not like the experience. He tells us that he is able to call his friends in the spirit world simply by thinking of them as everything is communicated telepathically. He gets a row off Albert then because he was saying something rude!

New male spirit. He tells us that he was born in South Africa in 1695 and is a white African. His name is Christen Van Hoyst. In 1703 his family emigrated to the USA to prospect for gold but they were never successful at it. He was 8 years old when they emigrated but he says that there are still generations of his family in South Africa. He tells us that his family's land in the USA was in the middle of a battle being fought between the Native Americans and the American soldiers, but that they as a family created a township/homestead and lived amongst the Indians. He tells us this to emphasise the point that no matter what your race, creed or colour you can live successfully together.

The township was called Mandeville. They had over 13,000 cattle. He describes the conditions as being very harsh but not unsimilar to their home in South Africa. He lived a long and happy life, passing away in 1774 at the age of 79. He tells us that his brothers and other siblings had left the homestead but he and his wife had stayed on the land but had downsized the farm. They didn't have any children of their own.

He explains that with him being white it was remarkable that his family had lived peacefully amongst the Native American chiefs but reminds us that history is not all that is written. He states that if we look at life through negative eyes it will bring us down. He warns us that at some time in our lives we will all hit rock bottom but we must realise that in comparison to some, our rock bottom will be someone else's high. We have so much and some have so little.

He says that in his family when the chips were down, his father did something about it – so we should ask ourselves what really is a bad day for us? He tells us to always smile because smiling is infectious and there is always someone worse off than us. He says that when someone is having a bad day they do not always show it, our words and actions can have a profound effect on them. Remember to be mindful of this and be kind always. He has to leave then and we invite him to join us again. He is very touched by this.

Albert returns. Albert tells us that it is important that we stop talking about the politics of the world and ask our communicators lots of questions about their experiences of their passing over. They are able to give us wonderful insights into the spirit world and the lives they are living there.

We tell Albert that we have got into the habit of thinking about him and conversing with him all of the time and not connecting so much to our own guides. He reminds us that we must talk to and listen to our own guides. He advises, *'You have to pull back the bond if you feel it has gone – but be assured, it will never be gone.'* We tell him that he is a great comfort and friend to us all.

He tells Ange that she is the inspiration behind the group and that he could come through any one of us. He wouldn't let Colin do that through the females in the group though! He reminds us that the people in the spirit world can see us on a big screen and it is wonderful for us and them. He advises us to meditate and sit in the quiet as much as possible to meet with our guides.

Tracey tells Albert about a wonderful experience she had earlier that day. She explained that she had been sitting out in her garden and had become very still and felt peace and joy and unconditional love for everything. She was made aware of a lovely energy drawing close to her and wondered if it had been one of her guides. Albert was able to confirm that it was her healing guide. She could see her guide through her third eye. He says, *'That guide was put there for a reason today, your pineal gland was cleared. because you took the time to relax. This will give your guides the chance to step in to say hello'*

Theresa asks to thank Tracey for what she had done for her and her mum and the love, care and support she had demonstrated. Albert praised her saying that she is *'a true model nurse.'*

Albert reminds us again that our development in trance is two-fold. *'You must say what you see.'* The spirit-beings need us to tell them what we can see as this strengthens the communication between us and confirms to them that what they are doing is correct. Earlier on in the trance session we had all seen orbs going up the wall outside of the box. He reminds us that we need to be looking around us as well as into the box.

SESSION 26
06.09.23

<u>Justine</u>

There is a light forming around Justine's head. A red band can be seen across the bridge of her nose and under her eyes. There is ***an old lady*** overshadowing Justine's face. It appears that she may have had a stroke due to the shape of her mouth as it was drooping on one side. She has small features, a pointy nose, old hands, appears oriental. She is not able to speak.

Another lady coming through. She has a small rounded form. Ange says that she knew this lady had been a fabulous cook, as she was able to see the apron on her that ties around the neck. She is not known to anyone in group.

A male spirit comes through then, he has high cheekbones, a beard and moustache. The red band remains across Justine's eyes. This gentleman is not known to anyone in group either.

Chris

There ***is a male spirit*** coming through. He says that he was the caretaker from Our Pete's school. He has come to give his love to Our Pete as he remembers him when he was a small boy. He says that Our Pete had always said hello to him when he saw him, even when it was not term time. He didn't have anything else to say so he left.

Matthew – comes through slowly, sucking on his pipe. He is still having difficulty with his speech which he is finding incredibly frustrating and annoying, he says it makes him want to swear! He says, *'The balance of energy is not quite right and that is also affecting my voice'*. It is very difficult to hear him.

He tells Justine, *'there is a lot of work going on behind the scenes to perfect the balance of the energies to help you in trance.'* He gives the analogy of using chemicals in a science experiment to get the effect desired. *'Each time you sit in trance they review what needs to be 'tweaked.'* They are trying to *'finalise your instruction manual!'* He acknowledges that they know that she is willing to work for spirit, and reassures her that once everything is in place she will work really well.

He tells us that there is a very powerful spirit energy coming from different realms and dimensions to give us healing. He tells us *'the energy required for these communications equates to that of a million batteries'* and reminds us not to take these things for granted. He then steps aside for the healer to come forward. Ange places her hands in Chris's hands to accept the healing and it is so powerful that the vocal resonations are felt by all of us. The healer appears to be pulling the unwanted energy out from us all and pushing in new vibrant healing energy.

A new female spirit – she says that her name is Angela Phillips and had lived in Swansea. She was a smoker and had throat cancer which had taken her over into the spirit world. Her husband was already in spirit. She tells us that she had worked for a while in Swansea library and had spent a lot of time walking on Swansea beach as she loved doing that. She has a son, a granddaughter and a daughter and they all live in Swansea. She says that she and her daughter were estranged and her daughter deeply regrets this now and wishes she had made things up with her mum before she died. She hears her daughters regrets when she thinks about her mum. She is waiting for her son and daughter to return to spirit themselves before she will reincarnate.

She is delighted to be able to speak in English again through a physical body, as communication in the spirit world is all by thought. She is amazed that she can feel (Chris's) teeth in her mouth and jokes that she wonders if they can come out! She says, *'I was a bit of a party animal in my time and liked a tot of whisky! And I loved a bacon sandwich.'* Because she had thought about it, she had created one and could feel meat in 'her' (Chris's) teeth, and is amazed by that. She describes how she was able to register her interest to take part in these communications with us, explaining it as *'like watching the adverts between the soaps and suddenly an invitation to participate in our communications came up. I was not doing anything else so I thought I may as well!'* I had a chat with my guides about how to behave during these communications - no swearing allowed!'

She compares the spirit world to the earth plane and told us that everything that we do, they have been doing forever, all of our ideas and achievements in the history of the earth plane came from the spirit world, through people such as Mozart, Sir Isaac Newton, Albert Einstein and millions more. One famous composer had said that the music he composed came to him through his intuition and played out in his mind and that he *'simply wrote down the notes.'* She reminds us that the spirit world IS THE REALITY and the earth plane is the DREAM. It was lovely to speak to her as she was very jovial and witty and was delighted to have taken part in tonight's trance session.

SESSION 27
04.10.23

Chris

Matthew. He tells us that he is demonstrating and proving his commitment to our spiritual development to Albert. In return his voice is getting clearer, but it is still difficult to understand him at this moment. He informs us that there is a curriculum that he must work through with us but Albert is not convinced that he is able to do this, so he is determined to prove him wrong.

Justine asks Matthew to clarify what he meant when he said about moving up and down tiers. He explains, *'this only happens when on the earth plane, not in the spirit world. I am going to take you through a guided meditation which will give you the answer to that question better than I can explain.'*

He tells us that he has received an offer to be reborn into this side of life, but is refusing at the moment as he has work to do first in the spirit world, to enable a smoother life for him when he does return. *'My last incarnation on the earth plane was very difficult. My mother disowned me when*

I was a 14 year old boy and I was exploited by devious individuals. I realised when I crossed back over to the spirit world that what had happened to me had been my destiny, and now I accept it. You must remember to be very mindful of the decisions you make in life, because everything is known in the spirit world, nothing goes unnoticed.'

He is asked to describe the environment he is currently in as he talks with us. He describes himself being in a classroom environment, such as the classroom that Albert teaches in. He admits to previously *'larking about and not doing what was required of me'* but now Albert is giving him the chance to prove himself, and he is very keen to do so. He encourages us as a group to work collectively together. Matthew tells Our Pete that he is a very talented spiritual worker but he is not showing how good he is. He encourages Our Pete to demonstrate his abilities more.

Paul

A new male spirit coming through. He is a very powerful native American Indian spirit. He is chanting prayers and giving us a blessing. We can see beads around his neck. It looks like smoke is coming from his chest and his shoulders, such is the power of his energy. He tells us his name is **White Wolf.** Albert says that there are many guides and helpers of the Native American tribes called by the same name, but this White Wolf has specifically asked to work with us. He has been attached to our group for a long time. We are very honoured.

Albert says that we are limited for time tonight as The Boy wants to do a table tilt. He says that they are going to work with us to do it.

Ange asks why so many young people in the world today are unhappy with the identity they were born with, and why they want to change their appearances so drastically. Albert explains that there is greater availability of opportunities to change their appearances now, from clothes and cosmetics to surgeries. He calls them all 'fads'. He says, *'When they return to the spirit world, they go back to the time when they were at their best on the earth plane. Vanity is a fad, short lived excitement. It does not last. In any life there is a male and a female but there is no harm in gender identity individuals expressing themselves as they want to be, but the media does not help as it promotes this way of thinking and the pharmaceutical industries benefit from being promoted by the media to sell their cosmetics, fillers and botox, hormone injections etc and gender changing surgeries. It is a rather synthetic world you live in.'*

Ange asks, 'If a soul is a female in a previous life, can they then be born as a male but still have the feelings of being a female?' Albert replies, *'It could possibly be true but usually to be indoctrinated into reincarnation they would go through the story of that incarnation first, their life story would firstly be explained to them. That story is task like, it is instantly forgotten on rebirth on to the earth plane, but when you get that feeling of something being familiar or 'rings a bell with me', it is your soul knocking on the door of your brain to remind you of the task that needs to be completed.'*

A new male spirit – he has not been through before, he is Japanese. He is a very happy spirit, and is smiling and laughing a lot, making us all laugh. His name is **Sang Lu**. He speaks to us in Japanese and laughs at the end of every sentence. His voice is very powerful and clear. He tries to speak in broken English but keeps laughing at himself and we are all laughing with him. He sings a little song and bursts out laughing. He gives us a blessing and says, *'When you go to battle, you and me will be side by side. We will walk hand in hand to battle. I am your strength. Life is the battle.'*

SESSION 28
25.10.23

Chris

Matthew. He is still experiencing difficulty with his voice. He is annoyed because he says his voice doesn't sound like that normally. It is because he is still being held back in what he wants to say. He has three learned friends with him who will work with him tonight to help raise the vibrations.

He wants to warn us about the dangers of the progress of Artificial Intelligence. He tells us, *'AI within a very short period of time will get to a point where they will be able to create events, they will cause significant tensions between powerful nations. AI has already gone beyond human intelligence and it will get out of control, there is a very real threat to you and your children and their children also and it is going to happen quicker than you think. The reason why they* (Albert and others) *are trying to block me is because they think that I speculate too much and that you should be finding your own ways through these challenges which is why you are on the earth plane. But I believe that you have a right to know, forewarned is forearmed. The way that technology has advanced, they can feed a script into a computer and that computer will act out that script in a human way, so you believe that you are watching a video of a human speaker, but you are not actually watching a human, and the difficulty is they can generate a video of one your leaders speaking but is it actually the leader speaking? Is that video genuine? It is going to get to a point where you will not be able to tell the difference. It is going to take control of your economy and finance systems.'*

Justine asks why this is being allowed to happen. Matthew replies that the governments of this day are trying to curb it. He states, *'It is one of your challenges as humanity, to tackle this collectively as one, because this will not be done by one single nation. Humanity has to come together as a whole before it's too late to stop this threat. If you don't come together soon, it is going to be too late and it will act far quicker than climate change or any other threat to humanity. Technology is used for everything nowadays and you rely on it to make decisions. For example, a patient has a scan, the doctor relies on the results to make decisions about the care that needs to be delivered. Artificial intelligence can manipulate the results and that will manipulate the care and the medication provided. All of your economy and financial systems are controlled by AI. The bank of England will generate the interest rate from a number of forecasts received by a computer, AI has started to inform those computers already, you need to be worried, you need to be researching. You can be informed by spirit, not many others have these opportunities. The rest is up to you.'*

He tells us that he doesn't want us to get depressed about it but advises us to **spread the word, plant the seed**. How this world looks in the future is up to us. Matthew reminds us that there is so much love and affection in the spirit world for all humanity, the world over, more than we can ever imagine.

Paul

White Eagle comes through**,** he is chanting and beating time with his foot. He has a lovely benevolent, gentle smile. He gave us prayers and a blessing and then leaves.

Albert. He tells us that there are two communicators with him tonight, ***Solomon*** and ***Rael,*** both are group guides. Rael is from South Africa and Solomon is from Greece. Solomon has been through several times before. Albert tells us that the reason they are with him tonight is because **they** are going to ask **us** the questions regarding our learning development. What do we each want from the group?

Albert asks Our Pete what he wants. Our Pete replies that he wants to develop his clairvoyance to get clearer and more concise communications. Albert tells him that they are going to set him a guide for this. He must call on her when he needs her, extra energy will be sent to him. Rael speaks then, telling Our Pete that this guides name is ***Chenille.*** He also advises Our Pete to call upon Chenille when he needs her energy, but warns him not to abuse her energy, only use it when he needs it because he is already so powerful. He tells him he must believe more in his abilities to communicate with the spirit world. Our Pete agrees to this.

Albert then asks Beth. She replies that she also wants to develop her clairvoyance, to give messages to help others. Albert tells her that they see her working as a private medium, doing one-to-one sessions. Rael tells her that in order to communicate properly she must firstly demonstrate her abilities amongst her peers. Her family and friends do not count as she knows them too well. Rael is going to be her guide and tells her that they will start with private readings as Jill does now. He tells her to choose her learning equipment carefully (i.e. her tools of communication, tarot cards). Beth tells him that she has chosen new tarot cards as she feels that the other ones she had were not working for her. Rael tells her to go with her gut feeling about her choice of cards.

Albert then tells Theresa that they have been sending her healing and she thanks them saying she is very grateful. She says that she wants to be able to see spirit as clearly as if looking at a living human being. Albert tells her that at the moment she must learn to appreciate that she can communicate with spirit. Solomon then speaks and tells her that she doesn't have to see everything in life and that hearing, smelling, touching and feeling are her first and most powerful attributes for her spiritual development and communication with spirit and are very important. He then asks her what she wants to do with her abilities; she tells him that she wants to help others. She tells him that she doesn't particularly like platform work, preferring one to one readings, and she loves healing and helping others. Solomon tells her that he will work with her but that he has to have her full commitment. She agrees to this. He tells her that they will not push her onto a path she does not want, but will push her on the path that she chooses. He says, *'When we push, we will push.'*

Albert tells Ange that there are opportunities for her to expand her class, but not within this circle as this circle is complete. (Albert describes our group as a gathering of family). He tells her to not contain herself either as she has so much to give. She tells Albert that she wants to achieve a higher level of ability with her teaching. He tells her that although she has two classes ongoing at the moment, they have noticed that she has spare capacity in her life! He tells her, *'You have not been doing any spiritual work yourself for a while, and in order to preach you must partake.'* She begins to protest and he tells her to *' stop making noise!'* He tells her to *'put out the feelers for a daytime class'* so that she can develop more as a teacher.

Albert asks Tracey what she wants, he tells her that she is one of his favourite students as she always has so much to say! He tells her that she knows her path, she's been told many times but continues to do very little about it. She tells him that she has bought many books on the subject of healing, which look very nice on her bookshelf! Albert replies, saying, *'The Boy owned a bicycle once – it looked very nice as a clothes hanger!'* He tells her to combine the healing with the herbal learning as they are **both very important.** Albert says he will bring his sister to help her, her name is **Chamillia.** She has Italian origins. She was a great healer in life, tending to soldiers in battles. She will step forward and Tracey must look out for her.

Gemma – Albert teases her saying, *'You sit in silence most evenings, but you are a very powerful lady, however you are only firing on 3 cylinders as you let your lack of confidence get in your way, you will flourish when you get over this. I will work with you.'* He tells her that he is great for getting confidence issues away from people and she is very happy about this.

Gemma tells him that she has been wondering if she should continue coming to the group to which we all react, telling her she must stay in the group. Rael speaks then saying, *'The element of doubt is caused by darkness trying to get into your head, we will banish that of course with your permission, but you have to be disciplined. Because the lack of confidence is the biggest thing in discipline, you almost have to be blasé about it. How many people have you told about your gift? I could count on one hand, but you should be telling everyone about it, they may look at you as if you have two heads but we know who the mad ones really are!'* Rael tells her that he is also going to work with her.

Chris – he says he wants a better understanding of 'What is the purpose of life, why are we here, why do we go through certain things, where do we go after life?' Albert tells him, *'The purpose of life is a lesson, but for spirituality keep doing what you are doing, you have a deep-rooted purpose for this group, you are one of the pylons that creates the energy for this group and the group as we now know it has not diminished in numbers over the last few months or grown because we have set the stone.'* He tells Chris *'You are a beacon of joy.'*

He says that they (spirit) were working with and supporting him and Paul on the rostrum last Sunday when they were giving a demonstration of mediumship in one of the spiritualist churches.

Albert then thanks Ange, saying that it is all down to her teaching, and giving us the confidence we need. He tells

Chris that what he wants they can help him achieve by bringing the right guide through for him. Ange starts to ask a question but Albert interrupts her saying *'Oh Christopher, your voice has changed, it must be the tablets you're taking!'*

Chris says that he wants more exposure to the platform, to be with like-minded people who don't judge, and to develop in a safe environment. Albert tells him that he will assign him a guide, by the name of **Emiray,** a Spanish guide who will come to Chris in his sleep-state. Albert says that he is going to test Chris, he must describe Emiray to Albert so that Albert will know that Chris has asked for him to make his presence known to him in his sleep-state.

Justine – Albert calls her young lady but then jokingly asks how she knew he was talking to her! She tells Albert that she wants to develop further in her clairvoyance, clairaudience and clairsentience to be the best that she can be. Albert tells her off for assuming that that was the question he was going to ask her. He tells us all that it is a life lesson, saying, *'familiarities can cost you, don't always anticipate similarities, don't assume'*. Albert asks her what she thinks is holding her back, and to share it with the group. She replies, 'Self-doubt and lack of confidence.' Albert agrees that is what is holding her back but says that she is quite confident and competent to do those things, she is 99.9% but not the full 100%.

Albert brings through **Cornelius Chambers** to speak to her. Ange asks if he had come through to see Chris! He replies that he has come to speak to Justine, *'but Chris is an added bonus!'* Cornelius says that he has noted that Justine is quite disturbed by what she is seeing on the news and how it affects her. *'You take it all on board.'* Justine agrees that is correct, Cornelius tells her to *'take it from an old journalist, don't believe everything you read and see.'* He tells her that she must have confidence and that he has bags of it to share. He tells her that he is going to bring someone through for her in a daydream state of consciousness, his name is **Raymond.** Cornelius says that on his passing he was introduced to Raymond who taught him a few things such as how to conduct himself. He gave him life choices as a lesson. He warns her, *'He is not one to be underestimated. Raymond can be rather impatient; when your mind wanders onto upsetting things, he will bring you out of your daydream state with a short, sharp shock! A kick up the backside!'* Cornelius tells her that when she lets her imagination run wild its always on the negative. Justine agrees that is true, she believes that she is not good enough or that she is not doing it properly. He says that he is not just talking about spirituality. When she thinks like this Raymond will come and give her a good sharp shock.

Albert returns – he asks how we think this session went, we all say that it was brilliant and we are all very grateful for the advice and the guides that have been brought through. He tells us that Cornelius volunteered himself to come through for Justine and to bring Raymond as well. She is very grateful for their input.

Gemma says that some of her family have seen a spirit walking around outside her mother-in-law's house. She has seen him herself. When they check outside there is no one to be seen. Albert say that he is getting the name Jason. Gemma explains that she knows that there was a young man who passed away a few years ago who lived nearby. Albert assures Gemma that Jason means no harm – he just wants to be part of another family, but they have nothing to worry about.

Justine asks Albert about the existence of criptids, such as Bigfoot, do they really exist and do they come from another dimension? Albert warns her not to read too much into the science fiction of it, it is much more likely to be a scientific or natural genetic mutation, possibly of a human being. But it is not a not a spirit-being.

Beth asks Albert if her mum has been received. He assures her that she was very much welcomed, she wants Beth to remember an incident with a pineapple (not the tinned variety!) in Beth's childhood. Her sister and father are also with her mum. Albert asks Beth to go out and buy a pineapple.

SESSION 29
15.11.23

Paul

A new male communicator comes through. He says in amazement, *'What do we have here?'* He's looking all around us and giggling. He tells us his name is Corporal **Franklyn Jones,** he was born in 1903 and passed in 1951 aged just 48. He states that he knows all about us from his learned friends (Albert and others). The overshadowing on The Boy's face highlights strange markings and we ask if he had been injured in battle. Franklyn confirms this and says he has many scars on his face. He says the injuries he sustained throughout WW2 had contributed to his passing. He had been a pilot in the RAF and was shot down. Unfortunately he had lost both his legs and had been confined to a wheelchair. We thank him for his sacrifice.

He had lived in Bridgenorth, England and had been married to Judith but they had not had any children due to his injuries. He had to come to terms with his injuries and stated that he was looked after in the POW camp, they did treat him fairly. He reminds us that *'Wars achieve nothing, it is a pointless task'*. He tells us that he walks with people in the spirit world that he fought against on the earth plane and states that there is no malice. He agrees that power and greed are the main reasons why wars are started.

He says, *'The soldiers fighting in the wars do so as it is their occupation and they fight to defend their King and country. I did not want to send people into battle but I had to, as a defender of the realm. You will never see a war like that again as in your time, it will all be done remotely.'* He states that we are involved in these types of scenarios in our current lives, such as the introduction of nuclear weapons and cyberattacks, and the introduction of pathogens and AI. He advises us to do our research on AI , explaining, *'you have to understand that there is always going to be evolution, this has been around since the creation of the earth, so when does human evolution run out? That is what you have to consider'*. He tells us that he is not the best person to ask about AI and there are many in the queue who will be able to inform us better.

He recently had a conversation with Brigadier John Samuel, who told him that he could come through to us but he hadn't believed him at first, although he admits that he had no reason to doubt the Brigadiers word. He tells us that his wife Judith is standing at his side there and we all say hello to her. She acknowledges that maybe one day she will be able to come through too. He states that he thinks it would be wonderful for the trance sessions to be held in a large auditorium to hold a large audience as its very rare that they have an opportunity to come through to get their messages across. He warns us that there will always be doubters, and newscasters would ridicule people. He calls them *'Pillocks of society, especially the people in power'*.

He has to leave then but says that he will come through again as he thinks that we are a very nice group. He says, *'Although you may see me in a wheelchair (he shows us himself sitting in a wheelchair as evidence) I am not like that now of course, I could run a marathon now!'* We tell him that we will think of him on Christmas day and he says that he could feel that sentiment. We thank him for his wonderful communication and tell him that he is very welcome to come through again to us.

The next communicator comes through, he is a ***powerful male energy***. He is beating out a rhythm with his foot and chanting. We know that he came to give us a blessing, and then he leaves.

Albert. He is blending into the energy, He tells us that he has missed us and we assure him that the feeling is mutual. He hears us calling for him when we need his advice and that he does look in on us from time to time as he likes to play games with us! He does not interfere, however, with our free will. He assures us that we are never alone and that there are many people on the spirit side following us all too.

Theresa tells Albert that she can see he is wearing a very vibrant suit tonight with a gold thread running through it, and Justine says that she can see his glasses perched on the end of his nose. He reminds us that they do like to wear these things to test our clairvoyance ability!

He tells Angela that she should be very proud of the development of the whole group under her guidance and teaching. He says, *'The balance of the classroom is significantly high as in high spirits and high respect for each other.'* We agree that we all have great respect and care for each other here on the earth plane and for those in the spirit world. He likes to remind us that *'if you can't say anything nice, say nothing at all,'* advice that we all abide by. *'If everyone took that approach, how much better the world would be.'*

He says he hopes he will be invited to our Christmas meal and we assure him that there will be a seat just for him. He jokes that he accompanied us on our Christmas meal last year and had been waiting for us to say, *'Raise a glass to Albert and nobody did!'* He likes a drop of Sherry and is also partial to a G&T.

He advises Our Pete to be confident in his abilities, reminding him that there is nothing to fear in a surrounding such as in our class with us, as we are a family. He says, *'CONFIDENCE IS KEY.'* He reminds us that everything is an experiment and that sometimes spirits do come in on an awkward frequency which makes it difficult for mediums to pick up. Also, the messages we are delivering are not our messages, if we could deliver even part of a message in a manner that they can be recognised by the recipient in the audience, then that's fine. However, he doesn't expect us to be flamboyant! When we do get a message which is jumbled up or difficult to understand, it is encouraging for those in the spirit world to see that we don't give up, we push through it and keep on asking for more information. Albert says that they are not specifically testing us but that everything is a test! Albert is well aware that we will be opening up to the public in a couple of weeks to give a demonstration of mediumship and he confirms that he and a multitude of spirit people will be there too.

Ange asks him if our future lives are already written in the Akashic records as well as our past lives. He confirms that they are. Our next lives are already mapped out if we should choose to accept them. Ange asks what would happen if she was to say that she doesn't want to reincarnate again and stay in spirit. Albert tells her that that is perfectly fine. She could choose to undertake her 'tasks' over there. He tells her that in the meantime she should embrace what she has here, in this world at this time. He tells her to look back five years and remember how challenging her life was then and how much she has achieved between then and now. The challenges that were put in front of her, she has broken through them. That is a lesson for us all.

He advises us to write down 10 realistic bucket list ideas and with a GREEN pen tick off the ones we have achieved. Green is for GO, for forging ahead.

He tells Justine that when there is enough information in the journal's writings and understandings, she must get it published. Then we will have time for vol 2 and 3 and 4 etc. It should be done soon. He tells us that **spreading the word** via publishing is the best form of communication. He reminds us to say what we see when the medium's face/body starts to become over-shadowed, this gives the communicators coming through the medium's confirmation that what they are doing is correct.

Colin. He is just popping in to say hello. He tells us that his mum has made the best ever pie today, reminding us that we can still smell and taste things in the spirit world if we want to. Tracey and Ange say that they can smell the warm pie. We say hello to Colins mum as she can hear us.

A very *powerful Japanese spirit* is coming through. We can see that he has a very long moustache. He says, *'Welcome'* in Japanese and keeps talking, but we cannot understand what he is saying although he speaks clearly. He then speaks in English and tells us that he has just given us a Tibetan blessing. His name is *Myuntee*. He is Ange's guide. He tells her, *'I have been with you for a long time. I worked with you when you gave healing. Although I am still your guide I stay in the background now because you are not actively giving healing, but I am with you when you are teaching.'*

He offers to share his guidance with us all when working. He gives us all healing, becoming immersed in the colour orange, which is radiating out to us all. His vocalising accompanying the healing resonates out and is felt by us all. The healing had a very emotional effect on Theresa, who is grieving for her recently departed family members.

Albert returns. He tells us, *'You need to understand that when someone around you loses someone who passes away, the simplest explanation that you can give them is to tell them that they have merely removed their physical body, it is as simple as that. However the timing of that comment is critical as they may not want to hear it at that point in time, but it really is as simple as that.'* He explains, *'The souls that you see coming through in clairvoyance evenings and spiritualist church services etc present themselves in their most familiar form as they were on the earth plane, in order for them to be recognised by the recipient of the communication. They do* *not look like that in the spirit world, however it is important to inform the congregation that sometimes the person coming through is showing himself as he/she wants to be recognised not necessarily how the recipient of the message may remember them. It goes over their heads sometimes as the whole experience of the communication can be overwhelming.'*

He reminds us to **Be Confident.** *'Confidence is essential BUT it doesn't come overnight. You have to do the work and attend the classes. You are all having equal input into the group. Remember to* ***TRUST THE PROCESS.'*** Albert tells us that they (spirit) can see the blessings being bestowed upon us by the energies from the higher levels of the spirit world. He describes them as glitter-like confetti showering over us, the colours are vibrant, it is like the most wonderful firework display we and the spirit-beings will ever see.

Theresa asks Albert if her mam is okay. He advises her to walk on the lawn in her bare feet and as she is doing this, her mam will be walking with her. She says that there is no feeling like it. Theresa asks if her mam is happy with how her possessions have been shared out among her family members. Albert replies, *'She has her own possessions in her mansion over here, everything that she loved on the earth plane is replicated. It's abundant, but you can keep the Showaddywaddy LPs! Do not waste your very vibrant and positive energy worrying about your mother, she is being cared for and is caring for others. She wants you to abide by her request to walk on the lawn with her as she wants to gloat that her lawn is better than yours.'*

Tracey tells Albert that we hope to take a trip to Oxford to look for his photograph on the wall in the University. Albert is pleased with this and says that he will come with us. As always, Albert reminds us to ' **KEEP THINGS POSITIVE.**'

SESSION 30
Xmas 23

Paul

A new male energy is coming through. He appears oriental and is chanting, giving us a blessing. Both of his hands are glowing bright orange. His name is **Mayagomein.** He is Paul's main guide.

Justine asks him to explain how a portal is created. He replies that the energies of both parties have to align, the split is mainly on the human side. He explains that spirit will always want to come back to talk and communicate but the spirit side only represents 20% of it. He warns us that, *'A portal can be created for the good, or the bad, what you will find is that positivity will draw more positive energies, negativity will draw negative energies. When the link is connected it is like a psychedelic storm. The 'storm' subsides and then the brightest of colours are drawn into it, almost like a galaxy.'* This is not something that any of us intend to do, but the question has been asked for the journal.

Albert. He tells us that he was standing with us when we opened up to the public. He advises Ange not to introduce us as students but as fellow mediums, saying that when she introduced us as students the audience's expectations dropped. He goes on to say, *'there were 17 of us here with you that night, walking around trying to nudge people and it was like trying to nudge sheep into a pen!'* He compliments Ange on how she had opened the evening by explaining everything to the audience, how it all works and what they could expect from the evening. Albert reassures Ange that he always stands by her when she teaches, to support her.

He elaborates more about portals, explaining, *'to create that link and get the portal to work is an extraordinary feat in itself, never mind in front of a crowd, you see.'* He tells Ange that an opportunity for her to work on the platform again is going to present itself to her and he advises her to grasp it with both hands. He says, *'You have an amazing ability to deliver messages. It would be absolutely lovely for me to stand in the audience and watch you work, showing how it is done. It would be an absolute privilege to see that and we (spirit) will fill the room.'* He says that her doing that would create a power bank for the rest of us. *'Little and often.'*

Albert is going to bring through ***Xii*** from The Legion to speak to us shortly. He urges us to ask questions as they appreciate the questions very much. He reminds us that they walk amongst us every day and states that sometimes they miss the feel and smell of our polluted world!

A powerful male energy comes through. He asks us to stand up and form a circle holding hands, including The Boy. He gives us a blessing and healing which is felt by us all through our joined hands. He tells us to visualise the colour gold spreading up our arms, and says that the presence of The Legion is with us now. It is extremely powerful. He asks us all to say what we experienced. We all describe similar experiences, the sensation of warm liquid gold going up our arms, some also experienced visualisations.

This blessing was given to us by ***Xii.*** He says that the healing will work for as long as we need it and before we go to sleep we must ask for the ***Ambassadors of The Legion*** to embrace us. We all know that we are assigned one Legion Ambassador each. He says, *'Visualise what you need, you* *are part of the Legion, the power of such is unfounded in your world. Thought belief is much stronger than you know'.* He promises us that he will return again to do the same.

Cornelius Chambers - He jokes that he is in a mischievous mood and Albert is standing nervously by his side with the Shepherd's Crook! He tells Justine that he has noticed a wonderful change in her thought processes over the last few weeks. He reminds us all, *'Never look back!'*

Ange asks if he had a life review when he returned to the spirit world, he confirmed that he did as it was played back to him. *'Everything is 100 miles an hour over here. It's true to say your life flashes before your eyes because it literally does. It is a similar process to watching a cine film in fast forward.'* He is momentarily distracted by another spirit-being asking him a question (probably Albert), he replies, *'I'll have it neat!'* We all laugh at this interaction.

We talk about the advancements in technology that are being made on a daily basis on the earth-plane. He tells us *'You, (the general public) are only shown a certain amount of technology that is available to you. There is much more than you will ever know about whilst you are still on the earth-plane.'*

He advises us, *'Think of The Legion and visualise them wrapping you up in a cloak of protection.'* He says that we have 'joined the gang' and that is considered a huge honour. He has met them on a modest level but is not a part of them and he wishes he was. He tells us, *'I cannot describe how proud I am that The Legion have chosen you and that you have been very privileged to have communicated with **Xii**. It is very important to listen to what Xii is saying to you, he is the most powerful being that you will ever meet.'* He jokes that as he is now a part of us he will *'slip in the back door, so to speak.'* He states that **'spirituality is not a religion, it is a movement.'**

Colin. Ange asks what happens when people go over to the spirit world but they don't realise that they can create anything they want, such as a lovely house, by just using their imaginations. He replies, *'Everyone is blessed with an imagination on returning to the spirit world, but who wants to have a house with 10 toilets in it? Anything can be created through thought, it's all about the strength of your mind.'* He says, *'I am as thick as shit!'* and gets told off by Albert. He jokes, *'Oh, he's off!'*

He tells us that he couldn't read or write when he was on the earth plane, but admits that had been mostly his doing. He explains that he was good at other things, he could work with his hands. He often comes down to the village (where he had lived on the earth plane) and has a walk around, because he can.

He tells us, *'Never wish what you have now on the earth plane away, because the longer you don't fulfil the lifespan, the more you have to learn when you come over, and the longer it will take you. So, if you think that when you come over you'll go running around the fields naked, with lovely flowers of every colour, as soon as you step off the train so to speak, you aren't doing it, because firstly you have a lesson or two about why you haven't fulfilled the tasks you were set to do in that life. Most of you have got dependents relying on you for one thing or another and you've got to look after them, but when your time is up and He flicks the switch, there is nothing you can do to stop it. So go with it, embrace your life, because as much as it's heaven crossing over, you won't come before your time. It's not a cruel world that you live in, it's a controlled world, controlled by the idiots than run you on your side.'*

Ange states that as human beings we use our arms and hands, legs and feet to enable us to do practically everything. She asks if spirit use their legs etc in the spirit world, or do they float or levitate? Colin replies, *'I've got two legs and I likes using them, but if Mam is shouting at me because I've done something wrong – I 'F***ing goes! Faster than Linford Christie, but my legs are not moving then.'*

He explains that they teach you how you can teleport anywhere. Ange says that when she comes out of her body at night it feels like her legs are on a bungee, one jump and she travels a huge distance with no effort. Colin tells her that it's 100% the same feeling when he teleports. He says that he will never reincarnate again, he is staying there with his mum and dad, and his brother will be joining them soon. He wishes us all a very Merry Christmas.

Albert returns. He tells us that it was Xii's idea to come through to us tonight and he has given us a cleansing. Albert asks us how we felt about the cleansing. We all state that we feel uplifted and feel like we're wrapped up in cotton wool. All the stresses and strains of the day have been washed away. Albert assures us that The Boy has also had it as well.

Albert tells Ange that her abilities as a teacher are phenomenal and it doesn't go unnoticed up there. She is very much missed as a working medium and he encourages her to start working again. He tells her that the best way to teach is by way of demonstrations to her students, and to arrange an evening of demonstrating her ability to the public. He tells her not to worry about the audience as 'they' will fill the room. He assures her that 'they' will be queuing up at the door for the opportunity to come through.

He tells us that he is conscious of the time so will take a few questions before he leaves as *'Cornelius is pouring the drinks!'*

Beth asks if her mum is okay following her passing and who she is with, has she had her first husband and her partner there with her in spirit? Albert reassures Beth that her mum is absolutely fine and that Beth's mum is with everybody and Beth's sister is also there with her. He goes on to say, *'I have to tell you about a parrot that has been appearing around them, it is a wonderful creature and greatly accepted over here by your family.'* Beth confirms that her mum did have a parrot called Mayna. He says, *'Three days ago you thought you heard a voice, can you recall this?'* Beth confirms that she had heard a familiar voice. Albert tells her, *'they had been calling you because you sent your thoughts out to them, they had received your thoughts and were responding to them. Although your thoughts were being sent out, as you weren't open as a collective to collect this information off them, they had to shout! Remember, keep sending the thoughts out, they will come back to you, you see, in abundance. You are very much missed, yes, they will come through to you from one of us in trance. When the time is right you will see them.'*

Albert warns us that at a time of loss, grief and heartbreak we can become very vulnerable. At this time we could let in entities that can change our perceptions and the way we think, so that we think what we are doing is wrong. He reminds us that we need to ask for the protection of The Legion and our spirit guides to block these entities out. *'This is very important. These entities will take any opportunity to creep in to your thought processes and they will use absolutely any method and most importantly grief, when your mind and your chemical balance of the brain is unbalanced, they will tip you over the edge with the balance in their favour. I will not let it happen. Let me tell you now, these people who are standing before me and to the left and the right of me in the classroom are all tutting* (It sounds like a rumble of thunder) *at the thought of these idiots trying to get into people's minds and create destruction, it's not on! Remember, the livelier and the more jolly you are, the more you work for the light my dears, the Word is being Spread. The healing given to you by Xii tonight was watched in the auditorium by us all. It was wonderful to see.'*

He then wishes us a lovely Christmas and we return the sentiment to all of our wonderful spirit friends.

SESSION 31
31.01.24

Chris

Matthew. We haven't been able to do trance for a couple of months because we have been undertaking other learning and development opportunities. His voice is still difficult to understand. He says he is still being held back from saying what he wants to. He reminds us that everything that happens on the earth-plane is because we have free will to make decisions that can affect everyone else.

He says, *'Every human spirit on the earth plane has free will, there is an element of fate and an element of things which are mapped out. Whether you are president, prime minister, king or queen or anyone else you have free will. There are things mapped out but regardless of who you are and whether decisions are big or small, you still have free will. The reason I and others are coming through to work with you is to try to assist you with that free will to make the right decisions. You may think that being a small collective of human spirits like yourselves, you can't make a difference but believe me, you can.'*

He mentions the event that we held recently, opening up to the public a few weeks ago to give a demonstration of mediumship. He reminds us that, *'The hall had been packed out with members of the public and that in itself can make a world of difference. You've got all the technology behind you. Just one voice can be heard by a thousand if not more, you've got the power of technology to help you* **SPREAD THE WORD.***'*

We agree that we do use technology to help us to do this, via social media, mobile phones etc. Angela asks what can we do to help to change all of the unrest and division in the world? He replies, *'The people that you call your leaders are all make believe, the title of king or queen, president or prime minister is a title that you have made there on the earth plane.'* He refers to the clock on the table saying, *'that clock tells the time, time is also something that you have created, there is no time, day, week, month or year in the spirit world, you have created all of these, it's not Wednesday 31st January 2024, it may be in your heads but these dates are all make believe. It's not that time, there is no time. There is no age, yet you celebrate a birthday once a year in your 'time'*

The name 'leaders' is a make believe name, it is something you have made up!'

He gives the analogy of putting ten people into a room, including a king, a queen and a president. They all take their clothes off, then no one knows who they are, no one would be able to tell the difference. They would all look the same. *'You have freedom of speech and freedom of will, you can do whatever you want to do.'* He tells us that he needs to put this next statement delicately. *'You are all here for a reason. One of the challenges in your lives is to put things right for the millions, and yet you sit here thinking you are powerless, YOU ARE POWERFUL. Look what you did when you opened up to the public. Look how many came in, by the droves, that's a start. You need to start spreading the message but in a way that they will believe you, you need to quickly write the journal and get it published, there are souls out there who don't necessarily believe or don't have the time in their lives for this kind of thing, they can read the book and this will help them believe.'*

Justine wants to clarify that the aim of the journal will be to spread the word about the existence of the afterlife and to help people realise that they are responsible for their own thoughts, words and actions in this life and how their behaviours affect other people mentally, physically and emotionally. It will not be about politics, religion or any other controversial subject. It may briefly touch on these things to highlight a point. It will hopefully encourage people to carry out their own research and come to their own conclusions. It will also hopefully give people knowledge and peace in their hearts and minds. Matthew says goodbye then.

A new, strong male spirit comes through, bringing healing for Jill on behalf of Chow Ling. He has brought two friends with him to join in with him and us in channelling healing energy to Jill. He doesn't tell us his name but gives us a little bit of information about his last life. He tells us he has been in spirit since 1947. He was born in Munich, Germany and travelled widely across most of Europe, his final days were spent in Switzerland. He was an upholsterer and he was also a martial artist. He is a very well-spoken gentleman. As we watch his hands we can see the light coming from his hands, his hands are bright orange, we can feel the strength of the energy resonating outwards. It is an incredible experience as always. We are very blessed and honoured.

A new female spirit comes through. She tells us that she is chewing strawberry flavoured gum. She says, *'I haven't had chewing gum since before I died!'* Her name is Lynda, she was born in Glasfryn in 1951 and died in 2015 age 64. She died from lung cancer. She says, *'This is all new, I put my name down four times to come through but now that I'm through it's all a bit strange!'*

She says that she is finding it difficult to differentiate between her last life and other lives before that and is confused trying to remember which life was which. She tells us that she has reincarnated 24 times. She says that she is seeing spirit lights everywhere and is turning Chris's head in all directions as she looks at these lights. She describes them as *'former humans.'*

She tells us that she is not actually speaking with her mouth, she is thinking about the words and the words are coming out of Chris's mouth as we are hearing them. She says, *'It's weird, with this person's eyes that I am borrowing, I can see walls and a roof over me.'* Ange explains that Chris is sitting in The Box (the box used for the trance sessions) and she says that she was wondering why she was in such a small room! We were all laughing at her amazement. She tells us *'When I look with my own eyes there are no walls, no roof, no floor, just spirit-beings everywhere'.*

Justine asks her if she can see her clearly. She replies, *'Well, with this person's eyes I can see you but you are more of a light being. You are a mix of red, green and yellow light, but I can see through you, and there are rows and rows of spirit as far as you can see. They are shaped like humans but they are light.'*

Gemma asks where she had lived in Llanelli, she replies that she had lived in Tumble, then Carmarthen and then returned to Llanelli. She tells us that she was hearing music (it was Ange's phone going off). She says goodbye then and leaves.

A male spirit quickly comes through then. He is gently humming and smiling. There are many glowing lights behind Chris. **Glyn Williams** introduces himself. He has been in spirit since 2002. He had lived in Cardigan for many years and states he was from a farming community. Ange asks if that is a Welsh name and he replies, *'It's Welsh, we're in bloody Wales!'* Although he was born in Cardigan he lived in Maen Clochog after he married. He used to have a stall in Caernarvon market once a month. He tells us that one day he was transporting a horse box and it came off the back of his lorry and when he looked, *'the bloody thing was rolling along beside me!'* We were all laughing but he tells us that he was not joking!

He tells us that it was amazing watching his own funeral, it was really nice for him to see everyone there and to hear the wonderful things they were saying about him but he regrets that it was not until then that he realised how highly thought of he was. He swears and gets told off by Albert. He tells us that he was being pulled back (probably with the Shepherd's Crook!). Ange points out that he has teeth missing, he's devastated at this and says, *'Oh shit! They told me that they'd come back when I came through mun!'* But he came through without the opportunity of getting his dentures in first!

He is saying that he has to come back to the earth plane but wants to wait until his son returns to the spirit world first. He tells us that his son is working his guts out and that if he reincarnated he would not be able to support him as he does now. *'He has the family farm and it's a tough game, him and his cousin working from dawn until dusk. I support him from this side, he doesn't know that of course, I even had to pull invoices out from the draw the other day and he came home and blamed everyone for moving papers but it was bloody me, wasn't it! But if I don't, he's going to get himself into a load of trouble. He's too blasé about things.'*

He tells us that he is currently going through the process of choosing his next life on the earth plane, he describes it as looking through a catalogue (we have been told of this 'catalogue' before) to see where he can get some bonus points that will help him make decisions about his choices, what will give him the best opportunities to complete his tasks and to be able to return back to the spirit world quicker. Life A could be more difficult but shorter, life B could be less difficult but longer. He states that if he is reborn into a third world country his lifetime on the earth plane will be short and conversely if he is born into a wealthier country it will be longer. Ange asks him if he likes his life in the spirit world. He replies, *'It is fantastic, blissful and amazing. There are no words in this world that can describe it. We live in colour and immense warmth. The greenery is like you have never seen before, the intensity of the colours is absolutely outstanding, and I'm talking about nothing your human eyes can ever capture. You look at these technologies and books and whatnots where they enhance things, well, it doesn't come close, not at all.'*

He tells us that he has almost forgotten how to speak in our language and method of speaking, as everything is communicated telepathically over there, and a method that spirit uses to communicate to us human beings is by way of putting impressions in our minds.

Ange asks if he lives in a house over there. He tells us that he doesn't live in a house as he is a farmer and doesn't feel it necessary as *'the land is the thing and I can do it all day and every day.'* He has a few things left to complete in the spirit world before he returns to the earth plane. He tells us, *'You all have guides that stick with you from start to finish, it's amazing, and when you come back over it's like you've never been away. They are family in essence.'*

He negotiates with his guides on deciding his next life's tasks. He tells us that he doesn't have many tasks left to do and when they are completed he won't have to return to the earth plane ever again, he can continue to live in the spirit world. He commiserates with us having to live through such a tough time on the earth plane, but reassures us by saying that they are around us all of the time as life in the spirit world runs parallel with ours. He says, *'Each life on the earth plane that you live is merely a blink of an eye in the grand scheme of things.'*

Theresa asks if they sleep in the spirit world. He says, *'The sleep state over here is like looking into a kaleidoscope pointing at the sun, but with the most blissful music you have ever heard. I like a glass of wine every now and then, but I don't need it, we don't have any cravings – that is a human experience.'*

Tracey asks if they are made aware of the times that their loved ones on the earth plane will return to the spirit world. He confirms that they are given an indication of it. He describes it as seeing in light when a loved one is due to return. He reminds us that there is 'no time' in the spirit world. He gets pulled back then as we have sadly run out of time.

SESSION 32
07.02.2024

Chris

Matthew is trying to come through but is really struggling to communicate as he is still being blocked. He reminds us all to SPREAD THE WORD. He is very frustrated as he is unable to talk, so he leaves.

Richard Morris – new male spirit. His voice is very quiet and whispery, it is quite difficult to hear him. He asks Our Pete to send him his energy because he's finding it difficult to communicate as the energy is a bit low. He says that he had become earthbound and wants to thank Our Pete for his help in crossing him over to the spirit world in 2006.

Ange asks him why he had become earthbound and he replies, *'My passing was a tremendous shock to myself and to my beloved daughter. I couldn't leave her. I died from cancer in my throat which had started in my lungs. My daughter's name is Hannah, she was 25 at the time of my passing. My brother is in Carmarthen hospital and hasn't long left to live. I have been around him a lot in the last few days trying to communicate with him, but I don't know if he can hear me as he is not indicating that he is aware of me. On my passing to spirit I did not know how to leave my body. I was determined not to go. When my daughter visited me in the hospital following my passing, I followed her when she left to go home. I was so connected to my human body that I had remained there for weeks. I had forgotten what it is like in the spirit world, because our memories of it are erased when we return to the earth plane.'*

He says that he had been having strokes towards the end of his life and is demonstrating a weakness down his left hand side and has a left facial droop. We can see these symptoms clearly. He says, *'I knew I shouldn't but I still wanted to have a fag!'* He doesn't want to come back here again saying, *'It's bloody hell there now!'* He states that the nurses there taking care of his brother are absolutely brilliant. He has to leave then. Ange recognises that he has lost some teeth and he jokes *'Yes, you can't get a dentist here for love nor money!'*

Paul

A strong powerful male energy comes through giving us a blessing. It is **White Eagle**. He is chanting in his Native American dialect. He says, *'I bestow upon you all a blessing.'* We all thank him and he leaves.

Albert. He states that he has been observing what is currently going on in our world and reminds us that we have all been given a free voice and need to use it. He states that he will do the same. He gives us permission to ask anything we feel we need to ask, saying, *'In order to protect you, we have to inform you.'*

Ange asks if Matthew will be able to communicate clearly with us again. Albert replies, *'Matthew will be given his free voice back soon, but first he has to learn to control the anger that backs up his feelings. The world you live in is a cruel world but it's not all doom and gloom, one must respect another's opinions whether they believe that they are right, wrong or irrational.'*

Albert asks us if we can see anything on his forehead. Theresa is first to say that she can see a big lump on his forehead, Albert confirms that he does indeed have a lump on his forehead as he had banged his head reaching up to the bookshelf! This observation is to test our clairvoyance ability as always.

Cornelius Chambers. He joins us to remind us of our role in this lifetime, which is to help others, encourage positivity, speak the truth and spread the word of the existence of the afterlife and the unconditional love of The Almighty. He reminds us that we have 'conscious belief' and encourages us all to always look at what we see and hear about everything in more than one perspective. He states, *'Nothing is as it may seem. You can believe anything you want to believe. It's all your OPINION.'*

He gives a simple analogy of looking at a penguin and seeing a penguin or seeing it as something else, purely because we can, it's all our own perspective. He is reminding us of this with regards to looking at what is happening in our world at this very moment. There are things going on 'behind the scenes' that we, the public, are not privy to, and even if we were, may seem unbelievable to us. His message is clear - ***'DON'T BELIEVE EVERYTHING YOU SEE, HEAR AND READ. Make your own minds up.'***

New male spirit – He tells us we need to look more closely at the overshadowing on The Boy's face before he introduces himself. He has some markings over his face but they are not very clear. He teasingly says, *'You talk to me and I'll talk to you!'* We all introduce ourselves and he bows his head and says, *'Good evening'* to us all individually. His name is **Marcelito**. He is Italian. He is struggling to keep his accent clear so that we can understand him. He says that he was a Doctor of Medicine in his last life on the earth plane. He had worked with herbal remedies but unfortunately the Romans did not like this and he was executed for his beliefs and his practices. The Romans had thought that his remedies and practice were unethical. He says, *'I have been asked to come through to you to speak of such matters.'*

Tracey asks if he was executed because he had found a cure for something. He confirmed that was true. The Romans didn't want him to share his knowledge, and he stated that many of his colleagues had been sent to their deaths for those reasons. He refused to give us any further details as he says that he would only give us information that would keep us safe. He did confirm though that it was a herbal remedy. Back when he was practicing, it was mainly herbal, alternative and complementary remedies that were being used as modern 'traditional' medicine was not available at this time.

Beth asks has anyone tried to do something similar in this current time? He replies that there are many remedies available today that are found in nature, but we are brainwashed into doubting these remedies and relying on pharmaceuticals.

Ange asks if there is going to be a shortage of current medications. He replies, *'There will never be a shortage of medication because it is all there to be grown! There will be a shortage of the artificial medications.'* He explains that modern medicines only block out a signal, they do not cure the cause. He encourages us to look for natural ingredients such as hemp, but grown differently, cultivating the whole product. *'The plant itself is what we used to call a miracle plant, it has benefits of both kinds you see, different tinctures can create a medicine so powerful for all ailments, it is a natural cure for everything. It doesn't matter how it is taken.'*

Ange asks if it would make her feel spaced out. He explains that modern medicine can also make you feel spaced out, but that is overlooked as it is labelled a 'controlled drug'.

He advises us to pay close attention to what lies are being spread in the name of GREED. **'SPREAD THE WORD AND SPEAK THE TRUTH. By spreading the word you will be opening up the avenues for others.'**

New spirit. Eric Harris – he is amazed at being able to come through. He says, *'Hello, bloody hell! They said you would be here! I can't believe this, I didn't think I would come through here!'* He tells us that in his last life he was a farmer in a small village near Swansea. He used to grow potatoes, but didn't keep animals. He tells us that he had been listening 'out there' (meaning the spirit world) and he had thought he was listening to a radio as he was hearing us speaking. He informed us that he had suffered a nasty head injury and had suffered a bleed on the brain. He was driving his tractor and hit a girder on the barn when he was driving into it. He didn't die directly from that but did suffer complications that related to his death four years later. He says that his memory had been badly affected and jokes, *'When you come over,* *there is no pain but they don't take the twpness out of you see!'*

His injury had left him with a stammer and he is demonstrating this to us, although of course he does not have this in the spirit world, he is demonstrating it purely for recognition purposes. Theresa tries to help him out with guessing what word he is trying to say and he tells her off. He can speak perfectly again now but just wanted to show us how his speech had been affected. He tells us that he was unable to look after the farm following the accident, so he had sold it and gone to live with his daughter. His wife had died before him and they were now reunited. He says that he had been told to tell us that he will come through again and will talk to us about growing things. *'That is why they want me to start talking to you. I could grow anything, except my willy!'* We all laugh but he gets told off by Albert for saying that!

Albert returns briefly to say goodbye and to end the session. He reminds us of the importance of listening to our 'gut feelings'. He states that thoughts from the higher beings are sent to him as they are sent to us. He says, *'We have all been* *given the permissions and blessings of Our Father. If I was following the wrong pathway I am sure that I would be corrected.'* By listening to our gut feelings we can be sure that we are doing the right thing.

SESSION 33
14.02.24

Paul

A powerful male energy comes through chanting a blessing. He is Native American Indian chief **White Owl.** The resonance of his chanting is so powerful it is vibrating through our bodies. He is Jill's guide and he is of the highest order.

Tracey asks if he was a Sioux Indian. He says, with authority, *'I am **STILL** a Sioux!'* He tells us that we have made him feel very welcome. He says, *'We have come to thank you for your healing for our spirit daughter. Continue in the same vein that you have always done, life's journey can be troublesome. We will join in your prayers.'* We had arranged to all sit quietly and send absent healing to our friend and her family and out into the world as a whole. We are honoured that they will join us for this much-needed healing.

Ange asks for reassurance about her son. White Owl says, *'We shall shine the light above him, fear not. Do not show your own fear, it would be like putting oil to a flame.*

Contact your own guides, they are better placed to answer your questions. I will bestow my powers upon you all. **I AM THE HIGHEST POWER.'**

Albert. There is a flow of white light above Paul's head. Albert reassures Ange saying that *'we have had a chat to the right channels, with regards to your son.'*

Justine asks if Paul's head was being pulled up and back in order to give his back some healing as Paul has been suffering with a bad back for a few weeks now. Albert confirms that they were indeed giving him healing.

Gemma states that she could see 3 shadows around Paul, and Albert confirms that she is correct.

Justine asks Albert if he had tried to channel through her in trance a couple of weeks ago and he also confirms this. He goes on to say, *'I will channel through each and every one of you that makes that attempt to do it. What we felt this side, Justine, was that you weren't prepared for it. As much as your mental state tells you that you are ready, sometimes your physical body just can't adjust enough for us to get in there to tweak a few things, you know, but it will come, I'm sure of it, look at the strides you've made already.'*

Ange asks Albert if she has any ability to do trance. He replies, *'Oh, absolutely my dear, there is no question about it, each and every one of you can do trance. I would say however, that the forces that are put on one's physical body can be quite harming and we are very tactful in how we approach that. Don't get me wrong, but there are spirit guides here that will give healing like a rhino! But we know how far to take it.'* He encourages Ange to 'dip her toe in the water.'

Albert tells us that there will be a lot of visual demonstrations tonight and reminds us to say what we see.

A ***Japanese spirit*** comes through, he speaks in fluent Japanese for a few moments, then speaks in broken English. His name is ***Xing Pi,*** he clarifies the spelling. He tells us, *'I used be a farmer, I enjoyed my life very much although it was very hard. I have come through to give you advice on learning how to grow food.'* He explains, *' The armies came and took my land, and the same thing is happening now.* (Our farmers are losing their land at this time. 20% of it has gone to plant trees in the name of climate change.) *There is only one reason for that, when you give a little, they take a lot.*

You, as a western civilisation have seen them put their foot in the door, then they shut everything off, and then they can control human life. They are controlling what you eat and what you drink, the two supplements in life you cannot survive without. The question you have to ask yourself is how can you stop it? Do it with the brain, not with the hands (meaning through positive and effective communication and compromise, not fighting and war and loss of life).

You will be fed information that will become normal. It's propaganda. When the armies came and took my land, they told me it was for the nation's benefit. Only the armies gained, they starved my fellow friends. Everyone will be forced to comply. Its already happening now, look what's happened over the last few years.' He has to leave then.

A new male spirit comes through. His name is **Nigel Howells,** he was born in 1928 and passed in 1974. He lived in Bridgwater originally. He tells us that he died through an act of surgical malpractice. He says, *'I was initially very angry about how I died but I have accepted it now and I no longer carry any ill feelings towards those I feel were responsible. I died during a routine surgical procedure* *where one of my main arteries was accidentally cut and I bled to death.'*

He tells us about his life review that he saw after he crossed over into the light and he understood that he could not hold on to anger, he had to let it all go. The reason that he has come through this evening is simply to communicate with us, he has never done this in any of his lives before.

Tracey asks him if he had believed in the afterlife in his last life. He replies, *'I had always believed that there was an Almighty Creator and we as a family had attended church religiously and enjoyed attending.'* He tells us that we must protect our liberties and part of those liberties are the way we conduct ourselves with our right of freedom of speech. He says, *'There are many liberties that can be taken from you but they can never really take your freedom of speech, but they can limit you. I keep an active mind on all sorts of things which are happening in your world and sometimes I just have to go for long walks to get away from it all. We walk amongst you, you see.'*

Ange asks Nigel to describe his experience of leaving his physical body. He says, *'I remember lifting out of my body and found myself in the corner of the room, I was looking at myself on the theatre table and the panic that was erupting amongst the 3 nurses and 2 doctors in the room who were trying to save my life.'* He acknowledges that although he said it was malpractice, he now realises that accidents do happen and that they did not do it deliberately.

He continues, *'On looking upon myself I knew that the time had come for me to die, but I was heartbroken for my wife and two children who were in the waiting room and were being told that I had died of a cardiac arrest. In my case, I did not run to the light like most do, I stuck around for some time because I was most annoyed! The truth had not been told and it never was. When my wife and children went home, I followed them and stayed for a few days. I didn't stay for my funeral because once the realisation occurred to me that I was not going to be able to join them in the physical form, that's when the panic began to set in, you see, because I thought I had missed the opportunity to be welcomed back into The Arms of the Lord, as I had always believed would happen, and I was trying to find The Light. I went looking for **It** and **It** followed me, you see. So, I took that choice to go. And then you go into the portal. I want you to ask your spirit guides and any other spirit that comes through of their* *experience because for me, it was the most exhilarating feeling one could ever have.'*

Ange tells him that she has been through that portal but before she reached the Light at the end of her tunnel she was pulled backwards and back into her physical body. He goes on to say, *'You must realise that your ability as a spirit is somewhat complex, if you don't realise what you can and can't do after the event of your passing, and the life review that you will immediately have ....* (he stops there and then continues with great delight) ... *I won't spoil the surprise!*

'But everywhere I went whilst still on the earth plane in spirit form, I went by foot, entering the tunnel to go to the Light is like going through a corrugated tube. That is what I experienced, it was multi coloured and multi-faceted, with the brightest and most beautiful colours, it was as if you could taste the colours. When I was still in my home in spirit form it felt like a lifetime but it was actually seconds. When I entered into the tunnel and was travelling towards the Light I was floating and being swept along at great speed. Your feet don't touch the floor, and if you are as fortunate as I believe I was, you will be able to see other souls that have also lost their lives travelling in their own individual tunnels

around you, they are in their thousands, and all going to the same destination hopefully. Then I reached my destination. I was welcomed by my Papa. I can still smell the sweet smoke of his pipe.'

Ange says that she believes that there are also many souls travelling in the opposite direction to enter their mother's womb ready to be born. Nigel confirms that this is true. They are in their individual tunnels too. *'I will say one thing, what I experienced, and you may have experienced this* (to Ange), *I just mentioned the colours but there is a remarkable musical sound which you can never distinguish and that alone is almost the draw, it is Angelic. I was once told it is akin to the angels wings.'*

He very mischievously refuses to discuss what happens next as he doesn't want to spoil the lovely surprise that we will all experience when we go home to the spirit world. He says that life's lessons are wonderful but he is 100% sure that he will not reincarnate back onto the earth plane. When we ask him why he doesn't want to reincarnate he explains that this is because he is very content where he is, but he goes on to say that there are hundreds of thousands of others that do choose to reincarnate for their own personal reasons.

He says, *'One thing I will say to you all, you don't realise how much of an experiment you are all undertaking in your lives. LIVE LIFE TO THE ABSOLUTE FULL, and when I say live life I mean it. Change anything that does not make you happy. My message is quite clear here. You talk about things like propaganda and the people who are behind that and even though I could speak to you about all that I have absolutely no desire to do so, and the reason for that is because it brings the vibration down and makes you unhappy, yet you do it ever so much from what I hear! If you focus your energy on what may never happen, you are not focusing on what you could be doing to make happen in this moment. If you do that in a positive way, then you will start to see change.*

'So instead of sending text messages with doom and gloom, send a happy thought, do it for a week my dear and you will find that by this time next week you will all be skipping into the class. It will raise the vibrations. Remember the things one sees with one's eyes, can you categorically say

for certain that the good is the good and the bad is the bad? No you cannot. Bad news is cancerous to the soul.'

Ange states, 'We need that light to shine, to emanate it, to expand it as high up and as wide as possible in and all around us, just keep focussing on that and pushing it out'.

Nigel replies to that, saying, *'I will give you an example. I may get shot down in flames and the Shepherd's Crook may come out!* (Albert is supervising by the side!) *But if you are talking about the Bright Light of The Almighty Lord, you have to show Him the Light in the first instance, because if you're showing doom and gloom you are showing the darkness, so if you show The Lord that there is a White Light we want to continue with that White Light because we want to be happy you see, then He will respond.'*

We tell Nigel that he has uplifted us all with his wise words and he tells us that it was why he came to speak to us. He jokes that we have no idea how nice it is to talk to someone who can't read his mind!

Just before he goes Justine asks him if on his return to the spirit world did he feel the love of his own father as he greeted him and did he also feel the love of The Almighty? He refuses to answer this again as he says that he doesn't want to spoil the surprise! But he does say, *'When I was a little boy I deliberately smashed 6 panes of glass in my father's greenhouse, that was reminded to me but it was never cast upon as a sin, you know, he made me pay for them but that was in the physical world, not the spiritual one. I dug so many potato beds that year!'*

We thank him for his insightful advice and wise words, he responds by saying, *'Just do one thing before I leave and that is to think of what happiness and sadness is. There is only one way to get rid of sadness and that is piece by piece by piece and replace it with something happy.'* He asks us how do we feel as a group collectively, if we could put our happiness on a pedestal as a percentage?

Justine replies 100% when we are all together. Everyone agrees and Ange says that she feels that he has touched her soul. He replies, *'You just need to understand one thing, you know about the good endorphins that are released through happiness with having good relationships, think of the butterflies you felt when you first met your one true love, think of the anticipation before your first intimate moment together, good endorphins yes? So why do you need negative ones? And why do you need unpleasant things in your life? Stop allowing yourself to have negative thoughts. And when you are brave enough to make those changes you will see a remarkable difference, so stop spreading propaganda and bad news and instead spread happiness and jokes.'* He has to go then but promises to come through again.

Albert returns – we thank Albert for such a wonderful evening and he says, *'You have to understand you see, I bring people through to try and lift the mood, I hope Nigel brought some closure and reassurance for some of you. It is much needed you see.'* He is pleased with our trance sessions becoming a more regular thing. He jokes, *'I will send up the red flags and get the invites out!'* He asks us to send out our thoughts and see who comes along. Before he leaves he says to us, *'you won't get higher than White Owl in this group.'* We are honoured.

SESSION 34
22.02.24

Justine

A new female spirit. She is showing herself clearly and we can see she is wearing large hoop earrings, She looks about 50 years of age. Paul can see two figures trying to show themselves at the same time which is resulting in the two spirit energies flashing in and out. Tracey says that the male energy reminds her of her brother.

Another female spirit comes through – she has black hair and is wearing glasses. Someone says that she looks like Hayley in Coronation street! There are lots of energies overshadowing Justine's face, two people are trying to come through at the same time again. Paul can clearly see energy behind Justine.

Another female spirit. Paul can see her clearly and he gets the impression that she was a bit of a free spirit. She appears to have a mole on the side of her left cheek. There is a younger person coming through. Paul thinks she may have been famous. Chris can see Angel wings behind Justine. Beth can see white light.

[Paul could see a montage of spirits that have come through this evening. In between the female spirits two male spirits had also overshadowed Justine.]

Paul

We can see lots of energy over Paul's shoulder and there are many colours in the box. There is a male spirit appearing, he has quite long dark hair with what appears to be a skull cap, he looks Jewish/Arabian. He is giving us a blessing. He tells us that his name is **Korin.** He confirms that he is from Israel.

Tracey asks if he has come through to speak about the troubles that are currently occurring in his homeland. He tells us that there has always been conflict in his country. He says that he is a visitor to our group, '*just passing through'*. He has nothing else to say so we tell him he is very welcome to drop in again if he wants to. He thanks us.

Albert. Beth notices that he is wearing a white shirt tonight. He tells us that there will be frequent visitors tonight and advises us not to squander opportunities to ask questions.

Chow Ling comes through. He has come to give us all healing. We stand in a circle with joined hands, holding Paul's hands to complete the circle for Chow Ling to pass the healing through. Tracey thanks Chow Ling for helping with healing for one of our dear friends and fellow medium who is unwell at this moment in time. The healing energy is extremely powerful. Chow Ling chants at the same time. There appears to be a beam of light coming from his finger. We thank him for the healing.

Ange asks in what shape or form he can see us. He replies that he can see us as shapes. Chris asks him if he misses being on the earth plane. He tells us, *'I do not miss being on the earth plane but you should not dismiss the lives you are leading. When you return, you will see your lives, you will see that you have choices, in spirit also. When we are reborn on the earth plane we leave loved ones in the spirit world but because there is no time in the spirit world it seems that we return there very quickly, even though in earth time it has been a lifetime.'*

An oriental male spirit comes through next, he is talking and laughing. His name is ***Xiang Po*** and he is from Singapore.

He tells Ange, *'I am come for you. You are not 'full power.'* He says that she is lacking in magnesium and zinc, they help the body absorb better and tells her she must take these. *'Your body will heal itself without the need for an operation. You need to go back to nature to find magnesium and zinc in the first instance.'*

A new male spirit comes through. He is a very big man. He tells us that he stands at 6'6.' His name is **Captain John Saunders.** Ange tells him that she can see that he has a very large build and he jokingly thanks her and says that he does not know whether to take that as a compliment! He was originally from Somerset, England but had been in the British army in his last life and was posted a lot overseas. He had spent 21 years in India where he had met his wife. They had no children but had many nieces and nephews. He tells us that he passed back into the spirit world in 1958 from general deterioration of the body as a result of old age.

He says, *'Everything was just breaking down at the end, but I had lived a wonderful life!'* He describes his passing over as a short experience, saying, *'I knew that the time was coming, I laid in a hospice bed for the last three weeks of my life and I was having frequent visitations from my father and mother, my grandparents and a comrade that I had served with so I knew my time was coming.'*

Tracey asks him if he had been scared of dying and of these visitations. He replies, *'Absolutely not, my dear, I was 83 years of age and I knew that life, as we know it, doesn't go on for ever.'*

Ange asks him if he ever considered that his 'visions' were induced by medications. He replies, *'No, I was in no pain towards the end, therefore I was not taking any strong painkillers. I was surrounded by my family and friends and suddenly I knew that the time had come because I could look back on them holding my hands as I drew my last breath on the earth plane. I was lifting out, looking back, I knew I didn't have to do anything much so I just walked towards a corner in the room, for some reason I was led there, in fact I was called there. I knew where to go and I had no nerves at all. I had fought in 3 wars and in comparison to that there was undeniably no fear of what was happening to me there. When you reach the ripe old age that I did you know that every day is a bonus. And I enjoyed my life on earth, I put it down to routine and discipline. Looking back on my passing into the spirit world, I saw the brightest light, it was party like, euphoric. Some of my comrades were there to greet me.'* He admits that up until the last few days of his life, he had been sceptical about the existence of the afterlife that awaited him.

Ange asks him what his dwelling place is like in the spirit world. He replies, *'It is much like the home I lived in on the earth plane, and it was there waiting for me.'* He explains, *'Our two worlds are very similar as they are parallel to each other, but in the spirit world there is no pain, no fear, no negativity, greed or malice.'* Ange asks him what he likes to do in his daily life in the spirit world. He replies, *'I like to walk amongst you, but otherwise not a lot.'*

Justine asks if wars are written in the Akashic records, as they are manmade. He replies that they are written as they are meant to be. He goes on to say, *'How they are started and about what type of war it is, is purely down to man. I had a wonderful life in the army but there is no such thing as an 'accidental war'. It is the way of the world unfortunately, wars have always been around for centuries, but every war is deliberate. They are planned by the powers that be.*

'Invasions of lands have been around since the beginning of time, you only have to look at the animal kingdom and how they mark and protect their territory; we are animals ourselves and we are territorial, we will fight to protect our land and others will fight to take it away from us. What gives a person the right to take someone else's land? It always results in a terrible waste of life, but it is principled. Did I enjoy sending my troops to defend land that I did not own myself? Of course not, but that is what you sign up for, for King and Country. War has deliberate actions caused by man for various reasons, most of those being greed and the want for power.'

Ange asks him if he has any desire to reincarnate. He replies, *'I have thought about it once or twice and although I am very happy where I am now I would never rule it out. I can just call upon the offer to reincarnate if and when I want to. I would seek advice from my guides and others who would help me to decide if the time was right for me to reincarnate. Although I had no knowledge of my spirit guides when I was on the earth plane, I recognised them straight away in the spirit world. It was like we had never been apart. As you know, all communication is non-verbal, it is all through* thought. *I found this quite uncanny at first as when I was in the military, the voice was often used as a weapon'.*

Ange asks him, if he were to reincarnate again, would his guides remain the same? He replies that he has no idea but will ask the question for her. Before he leaves he tells us, *' Everything that is to come is meant to be, but fear not. Just remember -* **To shine in the Light you have to be in the Light.**'

Colin. He has come through to lift the vibrations. He jokes *'That was a bloody blow to the mood, wasn't it!'*

Tracey asks him if he's been down to the village lately. He tells us, *'I goes down every morning at breakfast time. I miss the milkman, I was always nicking the milk! You always knew the ones that had done overtime because they had orange juice as well! We would go down the pub and have a lock in, by the time I would leave the pub the milk would be on the doorsteps. I'd be gagging for a drink so I would make a little hole in the foil tops and blame the birds!'*

As he always does, he makes us laugh and raises the vibrations. He says that he was only coming through for a couple of minutes and so says goodbye then.

A new female spirit comes through, she has a high pitched voice and she is crying and distraught. She is Chris's grandmother who has recently passed over. She wants to get a message through to her daughter but because she is so overcome with emotion she just says, *'Tell Helen I'm okay.'* Chris assures her that he will give the message to his mother. She seems happier then and left.

A new male spirit – He says, *'Hello, my name Is* **Norman Phillips***, I was born in 1949 and I was 43 when I passed in 1992, I was on a slippery slope, drinking and taking drugs. I lost my leg because of injecting. My family live in Swansea. I often visit my family but I don't think they are aware of me being there. I don't think that they would want me there. I was a right a***hole, see. I stole from them and everything. I'm not proud of it though.'*

He tells Our Pete that one of his family members goes to a church that Our Pete goes to and that he would like to make contact there if Our Pete will pass on the message for him. His mother and her friend go there. He would love to come back and put things right. He has been waiting to come through for ages but there is always a MASSIVE queue waiting. Albert allowed him to jump the queue tonight. Just as he was leaving he says, *'Cheers mush'*.

Albert returns – He confirms to Chris that it was his grandmother that had attempted to come through earlier but the energy hadn't been quite right because she had been too upset. He warns Chris that his mum will have a simple trip and fall which will temporarily affect her leg. Her mother will be helping this to heal from spirit side.

Tracey asks if someone with learning difficulties or disabilities will still have those disabilities on returning to the spirit world. Albert replies, *'No, on return to the spirit world you are re-programmed so to speak, no learning difficulties or disabilities will be present.'* Albert then bids us all farewell until the next time.

SESSION 35
06.03.24

Paul

A new male spirit. He has a very powerful energy and is chanting loudly, giving us a blessing, it is deeply resonating. He appears to be a Samurai soldier. We all thank him for his blessing and he leaves.

Albert. He agrees that we should video the trance sessions for Paul to see. He is looking forward to the golden ticket event. He has lots of communicators waiting to come through tonight. **Lung Tai** (a healer) is ready to come through, with his daughter **Mai Tai** who is also a healer. Ange sings a little song and Albert teases her about her singing. We are all laughing and this raises the vibrations well.

Justine asks Albert to explain how spirits can make objects apport. He explains, *'The concentration of energy is somewhat powerful to do that and if that happens it is because there is a symbolic reason for it, there are two versions of it happening. Spirit may be trying to prompt you about something, just to let you know that someone is there and also they do play games, spirit children are notorious for it. The amount of energy that is created to do such things is phenomenal and if you are fortunate to see it you will see it as a spectrum of colours and energies, you will see a blurred energy through your third eye. If you are very fortunate you may see the spirit that is doing it but that is a rarity. Spirits are very clever and will often do it without your knowing but you may catch it in the corner of your eye. It is known that there is no object that cannot be moved, regardless of size or weight.'* Albert jokes that moving television remote controls is his favourite. He says that if you are watching something on TV that he doesn't like he will turn it over!

Beth tells Albert that she sees flashes of red light in her chandelier light in her living room when the light is on. He tells her that she needs to look at it with her third eye as she is actually seeing spirit signs and not to doubt herself. Beth says that she is also hearing muted conversations when there is only her and her husband at home.

A new female spirit - Judith Harris. She tells us that she was born in 1912 and died in 1965. She died of natural general deterioration through old age. We can see that she has a gap in her front teeth, she has dark hair and is wearing a necklace. She explains that she used to be a medium herself, and was intrigued when she heard of our group. She used to host sessions in her parlour on a Sunday evening. There was an old lady who attended these parlour sessions named Eda Morris who was also a medium, and was doing trance-figuration back in the early days. Judith tells us that it was fascinating to see.

Judith moved to Oxford for her college years but hated it there and moved back to Wales as soon as she could. She tells us that mediumship was very much frowned upon back in her day and the Sunday sessions were kept secret and were only attended by her and 5 others, 3 men and 2 women to balance the energies. There was a stigma attached to mediumship then; she explains that she was a churchgoer but describes mediumship as her calling. There were many people demonstrating using tealeaves or cards but she was more directly connected to spirit.

Ange asks her what she thinks of mediums in our world at this time. She replies, *'There are people out there who are committed to the cause because it is a cause, however, there are a lot of charlatans out there too, just trying to get a name for themselves and to try and earn a living from it. My group never did it for monetary gain, we did it because we were connected, but you should however try and earn a living from it, because I know that your group is honourable, you are doing yourselves a dysfunction by not doing so. Why not celebrate what is now seen as the norm, it is no longer a secret, earn some pocket money from it.'* She says that she still dips her toe into several groups on the earth plane and enjoys watching mediums of all different levels and abilities.

Tracey asks Judith if her transition into the spirit world was easier for her as she had prior knowledge of the spirit world through her mediumistic abilities. She confirms that it was, but adds, *'When you transition back home everyone is treated the same, if it is a traumatic event some may take a little while to adjust, it is almost like a stunned feeling, but they know where to go if they want to go. Some people choose to stick around and make sense of the situation but I knew straight away (and you will get that calling before your time is actually up, you see) and I knew where I was going and transitioned smoothly. I had no doubt that I would.'*

Ange asks her if she has any desire to reincarnate. She replies that she wouldn't rule it out and had been asked several times if she wanted to return but she feels that she is *'not quite there yet',* in her own sense of capacity of learning. She would like to learn a little bit more and *'gain another notch on the bedpost so to speak.'*

Ange asks if there are people in the spirit world who like to take over and control everything and everyone around them as they are in this world. The short answer is, *'No, the people who thrive on empowerment are in your world. On transitioning back to the spirit world, they are immediately taught the lessons of life and that kind of behaviour is not allowed in the spirit realms. They are automatically reprogrammed (let's call it), to understand that there is no place up here for it. No inequality whatsoever.'* She has to go then, but says that her coming through and speaking to us has really empowered her *'to do some stuff up here!'* She says that she will come through again.

Lung Tai, a new male spirit - he is chanting and giving us healing. He asks us to stand up and join hands to receive the healing. He instructs us all to think about where to send the healing energy. He calls for his daughter **Mai Tai** to come and join in with the giving of the healing. He calls her his princess. He asks us if we have any questions for him.

Tracey asks if he was breathing in our negative energies during the healing but he says, *'No, I was taking in your ailments.'* He tells Justine *'You have blocked energy, I will free it, you must keep positive. Listen to **828Hz** frequency. This will help you.'*

He leaves then and his daughter Mai Tai joins us. We tell her that her father called her his princess, she likes this and is smiling broadly. Tracey asks how old she was when she passed into the spirit world. She says, *'I was a young girl, my father Lung Tai and I were killed by the emperor, because we had had served our purpose.'* She explained quite matter-of-factly that *'it was the done thing.'* She is building the healing energy and we are all feeling peaceful and entranced by her. She thanks us and then leaves after a few minutes.

A new male spirit comes through. His name is ***William Thomas.*** He was born in 1939 and died in 1979 aged 40. He tells us that he was a farmer and jokes, *'You can probably smell the horse s**t!'*

Ange asks what he thinks of what's going on in the farming world at the moment. He replies, *'They should cover the towns in s**t! Let me tell you now, they are robbing b*****ds for taking the land off the farmers in the name of climate change.'* He tells us that he died following an accident on the farm. *'I was paralysed after being caught in a farming machine. My father never forgave himself. He had always warned me not to be careless around machinery. Dad has only just passed at the age of 101. My mum is in the spirit world with us, she used to make ammunitions in the factories.'*

Unfortunately he has to leave then. We invite him to come through again if he gets the opportunity.

Cornelius Chambers – he tells us to stop chitter chattering and tell him what he is wearing. Tracey and Beth see him wearing a purple jacket with a pleated shirt. Cornelius tells Beth that she is on fire tonight with her vision. Ange sings

'This girl is on fire' and gets teased by Cornelius who calls her a wailing witch! He says that scarecrows will no longer be needed, just play the recording of Ange singing!

He asks us all a question, going around the room asking us in turn as instructed by Albert. He asks, *'What is your biggest fear?'*

Beth says that she is scared of the dark. He asks her how she can be scared of the dark when it is a part of the night? She says that she sleeps with the light on but he replies that she still closes her eyes. He will ask her guides to help her with her fear. He asks Beth to sit in darkness every night and to not be afraid. Albert had previously revealed that Beth had been a thief in a past life. It had been in the Roman times. She had only been a young girl but she had been imprisoned in a dark cave and left to die at age 15. This explains her fear in this life.

He then asks Gemma what is her greatest fear, she replies that it is falling and banging her head on a radiator. He tells her that in a past life she had been a maid in a country estate and had tripped over the dog and banged her head on the radiator causing her death. He tells her to put this fear to the back of her mind and he will ask her guides to help her with this to take the memory away. He also suggests that hypnotherapy may help her to eradicate this fear as it is from a previous life. She says that she has always suffered with headaches and Ange tells her that it is probably related to that fear and if she can control it, she may not have any more headaches.

He then asks Justine, she tells him she doesn't like spiders. He says that he will ask her guides to step forward and help her with that fear as there really is nothing to fear. He tells Justine that her grandmother is saying that she has the singing voice of an angel and that she is always in her thoughts. He tells her to think of the red chair, but she is unable to remember it.

He tells Tracey that she is in the same singing category as Ange! She says that she has no real fears and he tells her, *'You are a beautiful beacon of light, you beam positivity. Your aura is 4 times bigger than you think it is. I welcome seeing that.'*

Theresa states that she is afraid of underachieving or disappointing in everything she does. He tells her, *'You have never underachieved or disappointed. You have to do that one step, that is not a fear, it's an ambition. You have done everything you have set out to do apart from one thing, and that one thing is that you need to sell yourself more in the spirituality game.'* Theresa agrees that she is her own worst critic. Cornelius tells her that she must continue in the same vein as she is doing now.

Our Pete states that he has had fears this week but has overcome them. He is quite content. He believes that whatever fears he has there is always someone else worse off than him. Cornelius is very happy to hear this.

He asks Ange what her fears are, she says she fears nothing but he tells her that she is afraid of the unknown. They chat together about her fears in her sleep state such as 'Are they going to take me over to the spirit world tonight?' He tells her that she should only fear things that she can't control, but spirit will always be there with her so if she believes that they are always going to be there why fear it?

He says, *'Everyone has a fear of something, it is such a negative energy to have yet it builds your adrenaline. You've got to have that balance. However, swap the fear with something else. Get the same adrenaline buzz, go and do a good deed or something, if you do a good deed you will have the same adrenaline buzz so fear nothing, drive forward and leave it all behind you, so when you are questioning what is going on in the world, there is nothing to fear, because you can't do anything about it individually, but things are coming out, people are awakening my dear, and before you know it, the world is going to change for the better and that is because people are going to be brought to justice soon. That is something to look forward to.*

'What we must do is concentrate on **The Now**, *get up in the morning and build your energy chakras as they were meant to be built. Think of the positive outcomes of your work for instance, it pays for your free time and bills; bills will always be there so just think to yourself I'm going to go out today and smile at everyone. A huge difference can be made by a small gesture of kindness and if everyone did that the world would be a better place of course. FORGET THE FEAR, LIVE FOR NOW, CHANGE THE ADRENALINE TO SOMETHING GOOD. You all need to listen out for the sound of a harp, when you do hear it that is the time to ask the question that you want answered. It will happen.'*

Zhen. He tells us that he is from China, he has not been through before. He has come to give us an important message. He says, '*To walk in the Light, you must know what the Light is, you are all capable Light workers. Channel the energy to others around you. The Light will shine on The Boy, He is incredible, I am proud of him, he will be told and it will be shared through trance.*'

He tells Theresa that she didn't have healing earlier but that he will send healing to her tonight. He then says goodbye.

Albert returns. He is very pleased at how well the session has gone tonight. He tells us the trust is there and he has changed his way of working over there, with communicators coming through and that is to brief them beforehand. Hundreds are waiting to come through and they are all aware of the group. He is looking forward to the golden ticket event.

Justine mentions an experience she had years ago, walking up a golden staircase. She explains it in detail and Albert assures her that the experience was real. She was taking those souls to where they belong and she was chosen to do that. He says that experience almost glued her wings on for her. He says, '*People like yourselves will often experience such situations and you must allow it to happen. It was a wonderful experience. The people of the spirit realm will always take an opportunity to allow wonderful people like yourselves the opportunity to experience such events but we also know who and when. The Boy could do it every minute of the day because there is no fear, hence the theme of tonight. With yourselves, there is anticipation to do it but sometimes trepidation when it happens because you don't believe you can do it, but let me tell you now, you are chosen to do such things so don't let that Doubting Thomas bang the drum. Goodnight.'*

SESSION 36
13.03.24

Paul

White Eagle comes through, he is chanting, giving us prayers and a blessing. He says, *'Good evening.'* We thank him for the blessing. He invites us to ask him questions and says that he is honoured to be with us. He reminds us that ***'We are all One.'*** He speaks about the importance of looking after our beautiful planet but says sadly, *'So many of you walk on the land but do not realise what you walk on. The lands are the most powerful part of the world in which you live. You grow, you sow, you eat, you breathe. Why do you destroy such land?'*

Ange says that White Man stole land from the Native American people. He agrees and says, *'If it wasn't money, it was land.'* Ange states that Man continues to take land from the people under the name of climate change, taking the land to grow more trees. This is what is happening in our country and many other European countries at the moment. White Eagle agrees that this has always been done and it has always been observed by those in the spirit world. He states, *'It is*

GREED, *a small cog in a large machine, but many cogs of greed.'* He advises us to protect ourselves spiritually, and he promises that spirit will help those that seek it. *'When you ask for help, make sure that you are grounded. You need the land to ground yourselves. You, quite rightly so, live in fear of everything. Fear that is not needed in your time, because you own your own destinies. Your life's journeys are so prominent within this group, please ensure you fulfil them spiritually.'*

Tracey responds, saying, 'We will always ask spirit for guidance and help.' White Eagle replies, *'And us, you. Cast aside any doubt.'* Ange says, 'We're trying to tell The Boy that!' White Eagle replies, *'He knows, He is an impatient one. If only he knew.'*

Japanese male spirit, Xing Xi (sounds like Shing Shy). Beth can see a birthmark next to his nose on the left side. He tells us *'I was in charge of the horses of Emperor Yohito[1] for many years and I very much loved it. The Emperor had many horses, over 1,000. They were used for battles and farming. The emperor only ruled for a short time, he was just a boy,*

---

[1] Yohito may not be the correct name, as it was heard, not written down.

but I continued to serve the Emperor's family. I never married.'

Theresa asks if he has any communication with the Emperor in the spirit world. Xing Xii replies, *'Yes, but everybody equal unless they are teacher.'*

Ange asks if the Emperor took good care of him when he served the family. He replies, *'He fed and watered me and put roof over my head, what more do you want? I sleep with the horses.'* He tells us that he is now reunited with his family in the spirit world. He has no desire to reincarnate, saying, *'The time for me to come back would be never, unless I am told.'*

Beth tells him that she could see two white lights around him and he says that he has his horse with him. He has been through before with another group but this is his first visit to our group. He says, *'When the light shines bright we know something is happening'* meaning that he knew when he saw the light it was giving him the opportunity to come through.

Albert. He tells us that he has several roles in the spirit world including the meeting of new souls returning from the earth plane, particularly those who may have had a traumatic or unexpected death. He is there to help guide, educate softly and reassure them that things take care of themselves eventually on the earth plane. Albert says that many souls are very pleased to have returned to the spirit world, especially those who have lived long lives or had critical illnesses.

Tracey asks if returning souls have a period of rehabilitation. Albert replies that *'that would be decided on their return depending on what they may need and when they may need it. There are many individuals that come over that are in deep shock, let's just say, and that's where we come and nurture these people back into what really is the reality, but many who have been at end of life for a while are expecting to see something, so then it's not so much of a shock to them.'*

Tracey asks what happens to those people who have done terrible things on the earth plane. Albert replies, *'I don't have the misfortune of meeting with those fortunately. But they are nevertheless welcomed here. They have a chance to repent. But it will always depend on what they have done. The taking of someone else's life on the earth plane can be quite incidental, such as a soldier defending his life, his colleagues and his country. You cannot reprimand someone for doing that. But, for those evil people who do go out into the world to cause mayhem, maim and massacre for free will or greed, that is a different matter, and they will be dealt with accordingly. People see Heaven and Hell as up and down but it isn't quite like that, you see. Although all go to the light, those bad souls are met on the pathway to the light and are diverted away from the higher levels.'*

Tracey asks if there are any punishments and he replies, *'I can only speak from what has been told to me from souls who have repented.'*

Justine asks him what it is like in the lower levels and he replies that he doesn't know as he has never been in the lower levels.

Ange asks if it is only the victim who needs to forgive the perpetrator but Albert replies, ***'The Lord forgives.*** *The victim does not necessarily have to give their forgiveness also, the reason being is that someone may do something to someone that causes that person pain, perhaps in the heat of the moment, for example a drunken punch that causes another person to fall and hit his head resulting in his* *passing over, in those type of cases there is no pre-meditated intention to kill.'*

Ange asks Albert to clarify what happens when our lives are mapped out but for some reason things don't quite go to plan. Albert replies, *'Sometimes there are 'hiccups' which are normally down to free will, frequency and series of events; you can't really control that and unfortunately, some souls do return to the spirit world 'accidentally.'*

Justine asks what happens to people such as serial killers when they are born, are there events in their lives mapped out for them to become those evil people or are those traits in them at birth? Albert reminds us, *'You are creations with electromagnetic fields around your brains, sometimes there is a breakdown in the wiring for a moment or two, and that could be as a result of a series of events in your world that has triggered that, and sometimes these are the people who make these mistakes. No one is created to be a killer. The wiring sometimes is a little bit wrong. For argument's sake, if you think of the most notorious serial killer you can think of, he or she did not set out to be that serial killer, because they wouldn't have been created. But think of how many people live in your world, if everyone was perfect there would be nothing to learn. It's all about the teachings you see. And it's about these people who thrive on power and greed. Your brains consist of millions of electromagnetic energies, it only takes a little short in one, depending on the part of the brain it is, to trigger an event in that person's life, sending him or her on an unfortunate path. But rest assured when creation happens through the Lord's will, he will never send anyone back to the earth plane that is somebody without love.'*

Ange asks Albert his opinion on medications that could potentially cause harm. He says, *'The things that cause most of these illnesses and deficiencies in your bodies are your food supply and your poor water quality. What you have to understand is that the industries that produce your medications do only just that – produce medications, they do not produce a cure, whereas it is a known fact that everything in your world can be cured by nature. It is understanding that instead of relying on chemical medications, seek out natural remedies, they DO work.'*

He urges us all to look into alternative therapies as they provide the best treatments, medications and therapies and always have done so throughout history.

Justine mentions that many of the natural remedies known to man have been made illegal. Albert is quick to say that many are not, such as dandelion, lemon and cayenne pepper. He says, *'Unfortunately, again because of greed, highly effective natural pain killers such as opium and morphine from poppies are illegal as there is huge money to be made by those in control. If these could be grown openly and freely there would be no need for opioid based medications because you could grow your own.'* He then says, (tongue in cheek) *'If dandelion leaves cured everything, do you think you would be allowed to grow them then? You would not, and it's the same for cannabis, that is why it is illegal to grow it in this country.'*

Ange asks will our world ever change? Albert replies, *'Eventually there will be an exception to the rule, there is now in the USA where they are allowed to grow cannabis for 'medicinal purposes', it is actually allowed in this country but it is not advertised, of course.'* At this point Albert leaves to bring communicators through.

Peter Maguire, new male spirit. He is from Ireland. He tells us he died in 1983 aged 71 from Parkinson's disease. He is holding his body taut and rocking back and forth, demonstrating the Parkinson's symptoms he had suffered from. He also had difficulty speaking on the earth plane but now has a lovely Irish accent. He says that he invited himself in to speak to us. He recalls that he had the disease for many years and jokes that he couldn't hold a pint of Guinness for very long! As we can clearly see the overshadowing on his face Ange tells him he looks good for his age and he jokingly tells her to stop flirting with him. His wife is there in spirit with him. They have four children and six grandchildren, all of whom are still on the earth plane. He tells us that he wants to share with us something that he has learnt along the way, but teasingly says that he doesn't want to give all of his secrets away at once.

Before he reveals his occupation, as a test he asks us to look closely at him and use our sense of smell to work out what his occupation was. We all tried to guess but we were all wrong. He says that if we couldn't smell him then, we never would! He had been a fisherman. He didn't actually smell of fish!

Ange asks him if he worked with hops but he says, *'No, I just drank a lot of them!'* He gets a bit serious then, wanting to get his message across. He says, *'Some of you are wishing your lives away, when you are fortunate enough to have family around you that love you and want you to be around forever. Make them your priority, you know because let me tell you now, I used to go out on a Saturday morning on the boat with the Captain, and we would not return for four to five weeks, depending on what we caught, you know, some days we would catch nothing, some days we caught a lot of things and I'd be out there, I was only doing it to earn a few shillings and a guinea. It was a hard life but I loved it. I absolutely loved my life. I'll tell you now, that's what a lot of you don't do, you don't love your lives. You don't appreciate what you have got, and what you have got around you, you see.'*

Ange says that the climate we have here puts a lot of people off as we don't get long, hot summers. To that he replies, *'Well let me put this straight to you my dear,* (he stops and looks to the side to where Albert is standing and jokes that Albert knew he was about to swear and had given him a look) *you have to realise that what you said there is just a hurdle of life, and you have got to smash these hurdles down, because that is all they are, excuses not to enjoy it tomorrow. It helps to have a shilling in your pocket though.'*

Tracey asks if he was Catholic when he was on the earth plane as his faith wouldn't have supported the notion of spirituality. He agrees that he had not known anything about spirituality and that it was a *'BLOODY BIG SHOCK'* when he passed over.

Ange asks him what he is doing now that he is back in the spirit world. He replies, *'not a lot, my dear, I enjoy what I see and I walk amongst my family on the earth plane. I love to spend time with my family, sometimes they know I am there and sometimes they don't.'*

Gemma asks if he plays tricks on them, he replies, *'I'm not one to say just in case you bump into them, but we have fun, you know. What you've got to realise is that things happen around you, and maybe it will be me playing a trick on you, you know! Let me tell you now, your loved ones are around you as we are speaking now. They sit there and watch this and they are in absolute awe. You don't have to sit in the box to understand, you know. And let me tell you, let me tell you now, never squander the opportunity to talk to them because they want to hear your voices. Now understand this, over here it's all talking of the mind, but down there when we reach you, we like to hear your beautiful voices.'*

Tracey jokes, 'don't encourage Ange to sing' and he replies, *'If she wants to sing, she can sing. There isn't a voice that is discounted with me, you know.'*

Ange says that there is never a day gone by that she doesn't think of and talk to spirit. Peter acknowledges this and says, *'You all do, we hear your thoughts, but if you sense the presence of a loved one around you, you have to talk because they have missed hearing that beautiful voice. Although it's great to talk through the mind, there is nothing better than to hear the accent, because when you send your thoughts there is no accent attached you know.'*

Ange says, 'In spirit there is no barrier of understanding with the languages.' He agrees with this, saying, *'And I'll tell you for why, there was a Japanese man that came through earlier on and I had the pleasure of meeting with him, you could swear that I was speaking Japanese back to him because I understood every word he said and he understood every word I said. I don't know what he said in his mother tongue but I understood his thought process, you see. It is not a barrier in the spirit world.'* Ange invites Peter to come through next week in the golden ticket event.

Theresa comes into the room at this point, from holding a private tarot card reading with a member of the public. He tells Theresa that he must apologise to her as he had been curious to see what she had been doing, so he had stood behind her and looked over her shoulder and watched what she was doing. He compliments her saying that she had demonstrated herself very well. Theresa says that her client had been a difficult one and Peter agrees saying that the client had been *'always putting up all the blocks. We gave her a nudge every now and then.'*

Theresa says it had been hard and she had felt like giving it up. He tells her, *'That has been the theme of tonight, there are certain other people in this room that are questioning things and fed up with the tests but you all must power through these hurdles and obstacles whatever they are. Pass through them, it's easy enough to do.'* He is called to time then and says, *'It's been an absolute pleasure to speak to you all tonight and I would love for you to get your answers, you know.'*

New male spirit – Christopher Lansbury. He jokes to Our Pete that he is outnumbered by all the ladies and admits to being a bit overwhelmed himself. Ange tells him that he is communicating really well and he agrees, telling us that they have great teachers over there. He tells us that he was born in 1854 and died in 1901. He used to live in Bath and was a merchant shipmate. He was unmarried as his love was travelling the world with his job. He later became a trader in fruit and spices. He was often in the African and Indian regions but did not sail to the colder climates.

Ange asks him what he does in the spirit world now. He replies that he does not dwell in a house over there, he just relaxes and roams freely around, saying, *'Why settle down and live in one place? There are vast areas to explore in the spirit world and I have no ties. I like to walk amongst you as well. I am often seen in my home town by the locals. They see me as a solid figure, you wouldn't believe how many of us walk amongst you, even as we speak. You see a solid form but do not realise what you are looking at, you see. Quite often I am seen in my bowler hat. I am mentioned in the local newspaper under the headline Eccentric Gentleman Spotted Yet Again!'*

Ange states that in this day and age everyone rushes around in their busy, daily lives and do not take account of what they are really seeing.

Justine asks him if he would walk amongst us and when we see him, tip his bowler hat as acknowledgement. He agrees to do that and Beth says that we shall go up to him and say 'Hello Christopher.' He replies, *'That will do for me.'* Christopher acknowledges Our Pete again, commenting on how quiet he is, he says, *'He's an observer, but he is in a room full of women so he probably can't get a word in!'* He tells us that he has to go then, we invite him to come through again and he thanks us for that but says, *'You wouldn't believe how many people are waiting to come through, I am fortunate to have met many of them on my journey here and they are wonderful. There are your family members waiting there to come through also, It's quite encouraging, there is a level of balance, you see, of trust, and it has to be absolutely spot on because when it happens and you recognise them you will be mind-blown. I bid you all farewell.'* Before he leaves he tips his bowler hat.

Colin. He tells us that he has planted his tomato seeds, *'A little bit early but it's okay.'* Tracey comments that she hopes that the frost won't get them to which he replies, *'We don't get frost up here, you header!'* He jokes, *'When I was down there we used to nick all the bamboos in Aberdare park, there was a big bamboo bush there and we used to nick them all for the runner beans. On bonfire night we used to go around the valley and nick every bit of wood we could find. Mrs Jones would be screaming 'He's done it again, he's nicked our gate!' I was always the 'guy' in penny for the guy!'*

He thinks back and says, *'All of our traditions have vanished, it's very sad. There was a solicitor who lived down the road from us who had a big garden with an apple tree and we used to go there nicking his apples. I was up the tree one day and I heard someone shouting "Colin Jones, get down here now!" It was the local bobby, Peter Jones his name was, he gave me such a wallop over my head I never went back there again. That's how we were disciplined then, not like now. But I know he had apple pie! We used to pick the blackberries as well and sell them to all the old age pensioners for a halfpenny, we'd put all the green and red ones in the container with the black ones on the top! We used to have so much fun, you lot need to be having fun too because you need to bring laughter into your lives.'*

Ange asks if Colin has any desire to meet a partner in the spirit world. He replies, *'Courting is allowed. You can choose your time to meet a new partner here if you want to but I'll wait, like I did on the earth plane, for the right time.'* He reminds us that the whole reason why we are all here is all about **LOVE.** He teases Ange saying that she can't wait to get there to meet a chap like him! He tells us a story about his Auntie.

'I always remember my auntie coming around to the house f'ing and blinding to my mother, telling her about my uncle Graeme. Oh my God she said, since he's retired all he wants to do is have nookie! I'll be bending over dusting the skirting boards and he'd be trying it there, I'd be out in the kitchen washing the dishes and he'd be trying it there. My mother said to her that there was nothing wrong with that, it is human nature. My aunt agreed saying Yes I know, but the other day I was bending over to get something from the deep freeze and he tried it again. My mother said there's nothing wrong with that, he's just a virile man. My auntie said yes, but I was in the middle of the Co-op!' We were all laughing.

He says, *'Diolch yn Fawr!'* (Thank you very much) as he is leaving.

Albert returns. He tells us that Colin was nagging to come through. Justine asks him if he is still trying to pull Colin away with the Shepherd's Crook when he swears, but Albert now allows him to swear a bit as none of us mind, and that these communications are not part of a religious service. He is quick to defend Colin saying, *'Colin is not as Twp as he makes out! He is an absolute character and he has been by my side for a long time. He is within the circle of my friends.'* This is a huge compliment for Colin. *'Whenever you need cheering up I send him in and there are other characters of the same ilk that I will bring through as well. You will be delighted to meet them.'* He pretends to be stern then, saying, *'There will not be any singing!'* He reminds us to look to nature for the answers to our ailments and problems and tells us not to be frightened to use them, assuring us that there is 100% the right plant to heal everything.

SESSION 37
20.03.24
Golden Ticket Night

Paul (The Boy) is the only medium being used as a channel for this important event.

There is a ***strong, powerful male spirit*** coming through. He appears oriental and he is giving us a blessing. His name is ***Xii Jong Ping.*** This is the first time he has come through. He tells us that he is blessed to be in our presence and we return the sentiment. He asks us what it is we need to know. **He says, 'I am the guide of your guides.'** He is from a very high level.

Ange asks a question for one of us: 'Is my dad at peace and not annoyed with me for interfering in his medical care?' Xii Jong replies, *'All souls that cross over are at peace. There is no malice, only an appreciation of what you have done throughout your lifetime with them, rest assured they are with you, always.'*

Albert. He says, *'Good evening visitors and welcome. It is an honour, we have been waiting for this moment for such a long time and we feel that we have the right energies amongst us. It is nice to see PR present this evening, it's been a long time. Your guests are all sitting there now, wondering what on earth is going on. It will be lovely for the visitors to see and acknowledge that they see the visualisations. Let me hear your voices please.'*

He compliments Ange's friend Jackie on being a fantastic Lightworker. Albert asks Tracey if she has listened to the advice that she has been given over the last couple of years (regarding her journey of learning about natural remedies), she replies no and he says, (teasing her but also telling her off a bit!) that he wanted everyone to know that!

Ange asks another question on behalf of another of our guests: 'Someone has done a renovation on a building and feels that since that time has had a lot of bad luck.' Albert replies, *'When one works with buildings and such, they contain energy as you know, no matter how deep you break those energies or break the physical energy of that building you will never release the spirit energy. Spirit energy is connected until it is asked to go away, so unless you have* *appointed a medium to go and carry out an exercise, that spirit will remain with you and protect you at all times. Buildings live and breathe just like us human beings. So no, your bad luck is in your thoughts unfortunately, when you dwell upon the negative you will only attract negative energies around you, so always think positively, make this a fresh start in your thinking. I have told you many times about this, it is time to educate those around us that **negativity will only attract negativity – it is a Law of the Universe.**'*

Justine tells Albert about a lovely experience she had earlier in the week as she was waking up. She was aware that she was becoming awake and heard the very distinctive sound of 3 pure tones struck on an instrument such as a Tibetan Tingsha Cymbal bell. She was wondering why she had heard them as she was positive it was an experience and not a dream. Albert smiles and teases her, telling her that it was probably her alarm clock, but then says, *'Hold onto that memory, my dear, because you will experience such events again.'*

Ange asks another question for another guest. 'Are mum and Rita okay in the spirit world?' Albert replies, *'Yes they are, they come back with love for both of you, and they would like Theresa to go and check out her knee. Nothing to worry about but in the forthcoming weeks it is going to annoy you somewhat, and you can't fix it yourself. That is what I am being told. I hope that reassures you.'*

One of the guests asks Albert to ask her father who is in spirit if he has any advice to give her on her mother at this present time. Albert says, *'Please take baby steps when it comes to your mother. There will be a situation that you will find fearful, that situation is not to be discounted as a negative. You must turn that into a positive. There is apprehension about her medication, she must take it but remember that medication is not the cure.'* (She has recently been diagnosed with the onset of Alzheimer's Disease.) *'With illnesses such as Alzheimer's and Parkinson's etc, although the body decays and fades away the love grows stronger. Never forget that, no matter how much they will look back into their minds, that love can never be taken away. You are stronger than you think, but you don't yet know it. There are people you can talk to, not just in spirit - family and friends - on how to achieve a plan, you MUST do so and not take all of the burden yourself. Your father will be there as well to give you the support you need. Bless you.'*

He tells us that there are many family members waiting to come through but are not willing to step forward just yet. He says, *'This is an experience for them as it is for you.'* He is going to bring communicators through now.

Colin. Ange says that he's not blending his energy in yet and he tells her off for rushing him. *'Hang on a minute mun!'* He tells us that he has got his best suit on for this occasion.

Hayley tells him that she is from the valleys too. He asks her which valley and when she replies Mountain Ash, he laughs and says, *'What a s**thole!'* We are all laughing. He says, *'I'm only joking love.'* He is laughing as well. He says, *'It could be worse, it could be Aberdare!'* He reminds us that he is from Porth – *'proper valleys see! I've got to be on my best behaviour tonight, he's told me.'* (Albert). *I'm not allowed to swear, hello, there's lots of chicks here!'* Colin always lifts the vibrations by making us laugh, he is so funny.

Justine asks him how his tomatoes are coming along. He *replies, 'Well now, you've never seen such red tomatoes, best you've ever seen.'*

Ange says, 'Is it?' He replies jokingly, *'No, because they haven't grown yet, I only put the seeds in last week, didn't I? So, this is it, this is what we've been waiting for.'*

Theresa asks how Colin's mam is. He says, *'Mam is marvellous, still gives me the odd clip see, never too big to go over her knee she says, she'll have a big shock if I did! Remember I was telling you about nicking the milk?'* He stops then and looks at Justine's son Liam, he teases him by saying *'He wouldn't nick the milk, he'd more likely nick my car!'* He goes on to say, *'She sits in here,* (referring to Justine who is also a developing trance medium) *we've seen a beard on her, she's still got one on now!'* Everyone is laughing.

He asks if all of the guests are happy with what they are seeing, saying, *'This is extraordinary for us* (Spirit) *see, and don't let me frighten you.'* He offers to answer some questions so Ange asks on behalf of another guest 'Are we going to move house?' He says, *'If you want to move house, bloody do it then, what are you asking me for? I'm not the estate agents, I'm not on commission. But seriously, if you put your mind to it you can achieve anything. I wish I had learnt that when I was down there with you lot. Up here you only have to think it. Go for the best that you can possibly get for the money that you can afford to spend. Look forwards, not backwards and think positively, not negatively. When you think those three things, anything can happen.'* He says goodbye then.

Cornelius Chambers. He appears to be wearing a fur coat and a scarf. He sees PR and says teasingly, *'Well hello sailor!'* He then sees Liam and Dan and says, *'Well hello!'* He encourages our guests (He calls them newbies) to say what they see.

PR asks Cornelius what his profession was on the earth plane. Cornelius replies, *'I was a truth speaking investigative journalist.'* PR asks how long he has been over in the spirit world and Cornelius jokes *'Too long, now that I've seen you are over there!'* He teases Liam and Dan about their beards, saying that they were very attractive and that in all honesty PR is too old for him! He jokes that Dan and Cornelius as a couple does not have the same ring to it as Chris and Cornelius! (Unfortunately Chris is not with us tonight.)

PR asks Cornelius what his views are on the world as it is now. Cornelius replies, *'Lies and Greed and Power my friend. And what you have got to understand is that there are people who are trying to out these people, but the minute you break the seal they close ranks you see, and there are a lot of people out there* (general public) *who don't realise that you walk in the shadows of liars, you see. Not everyone is a liar, everyone in this room is wonderful, I can tell, but on the earth plane as it is and as it always has been, there is this constant need for Power, Greed and Attention. In all walks of life, every creed, every colour, every religion, you just have to bear with it, unfortunately the greed becomes more powerful and the powerful become more greedy. That's the circle you have to break. Best of luck trying to do that. Just look at what is happening in other parts of the world where people are standing up against tyranny, are they getting anywhere?'*

He tells us that he went to Paris yesterday, actively looking for the protests out there and confirms that they are ongoing, but he asks us if we are seeing them in our news. Unfortunately we are not. He says, *'There are active protests going on all around Europe and not just the farmers, but you are not seeing it on your news, you are almost living in North Korea. They will only show you what they want you to see.'*

Theresa asks Cornelius, 'Can you give me the code word that my mother and I agreed on before she passed?'

Cornelius is not able to do that at this moment in time but asks Theresa's aunt (who is an invited member of our audience tonight) if she is Theresa's mothers sister? She confirms that she is and Cornelius tells her *'She says she is always with you, will you light a candle for her a week Sunday (Easter Sunday)?'* She is deeply moved and agrees to do that in her memory. Cornelius then leaves.

*A **Chinese male spirit*** comes through. He has not been through before but he tells us that he is a guide. He doesn't give us his name at this point in time. He is chanting and is giving us a blessing but then leaves. He will come through again another time.

Another new male spirit – His name is **Didonshcoom.** He is from Cameroon. His dark skin is evident by the overshadowing on his face and we can see his tribal markings. He appears to be a very strong, powerful man. He says that he has been in spirit a very long time and has been waiting a long time to come through. He tells us that it is his first opportunity to come through and says, in broken English, *'It is very good.'* He says that he is very happy to see us and that he sees us all in varying shades of different colours.

Justine asks why do the colours vary? He replies, *'Your energies are different.'* He sings us a song in his native language. He says that he comes with knowledge to give us, and tells us a little bit about his life on the earth plane. *'The men hunted and the women looked after the babies. I was the head of the tribe and had many wives and children.'*

Ange asks him if it was a hard life for him as it was so hot. He replies that the heat didn't worry him as he lived with it all of his life and he was accustomed to it. Ange says that if she lived there she would be sunbathing all the time. He teases her saying *'You would be dinner! Your colour is not the same as mine, so you would be eaten!'* He laughs at us all laughing at that. Ange asks if he would like to reincarnate but he says, *'My land is very different now... It would not be the same.'*

He tells us he likes to walk around in the spirit world as it is so vast and beautiful. Justine asks him to describe the colours that he sees in the spirit world, he replies that he can taste and smell the colours as they are so vibrant and beautiful. He reminds us to appreciate what we have in our lives now, saying that our lives now are very materialistic in comparison to his, he had nothing materially but his family and his tribal members were everything to him and he considered himself rich beyond words. He knew no different but to live off the land and respect the land and the animals. He is so inspirational. He promises to come through again and then leaves.

A new male spirit - Gwyn Jenkins. He comes through laughing, he tells us that he can't believe what he is seeing. He used to live in Ravenhill in Swansea. Tracey tells him that she used to live down the bottom of Middle Road and he jokes, *'That's Gendros love, the rough part!'* Justine asks him where he lived in Ravenhill. He jokes, *'Do you know the bus station? About 6 houses down from there, I didn't live there!'* Justine says, 'There's no houses there.' He replies, *'I know!'*

He tells us he was born in 1923 and died in 2004. He says that he had lived a good life but wouldn't come back to the earth plane for all the money in the world. He is very happy in the spirit world. He describes his experience of passing over. *'One minute I was sitting there, right, and the* next minute, I wasn't. I think I must have had a heart attack. I was putting a log on the fire and that was the last thing I knew.'

Ange asks him what the actual passing was like. He replies, *'I have actually spoken to people up here and nearly everyone has a different story to tell. My experience was that I just floated up in the air, there was no light or nothing, just floated up, and the next thing my old man was there. I'll tell you now, the words he said: 'Welcome Home Boy' and then my mother came, see.'*

Justine asks if he was then met by his guides to which he replies, *'Aye, I didn't have a life review as such but they told me how good or bad I had been. I didn't see my life up on a big screen, just a finger wagging at me most of the time! Everybody has a slightly different experience, because we are all individuals, see.'*

Ange asks him what he first thought when he realised that he didn't have a physical body anymore. He explains, *'It was like pulling the plug out of the TV and then plugging it straight back in and instantly knowing everything, and that a physical body is no longer needed or required.'*

Justine asks him what emotions he experienced on realising he was Home. He replies, *'There is an enormous sense of warmth, which is strange as usually spirit works on a very cold vibration. But I felt the complete opposite. It felt like I was going on holiday, and I don't mean to Neath! You couldn't put a measure on the wonderful warm feeling, it was like the feeling you get when you meet your first love but 1,000,000 better.'*

Ange asks him what he is doing now in the spirit world, he says, *'Bugger all, I just like to be on my own, what I did down there I do up here, because you can choose, see. I don't go collecting scrap mind, there's no bloody scrap up here unless you take those Gates you know what I mean! I had no belief in the afterlife when I was on the earth plane. I was a grumpy sod then and I'm still a grumpy sod now! As I said, I was a scrapman on the earth plane, not of the traveller community though! We had our little wagon but my old man had a horse and cart at one stage, we were like Steptoe and Son! We used to make money out of nothing. I'm telling you now, and this is what you lot need to do, right, if you want something, stop asking for it and go and get it.'*

Dan asks if Gwyn remembers Blaen y Maes (an area of poverty and deprivation in Swansea, as this is where he was born). Gwyn jokes, *'Who doesn't! Nice place that is, twinned with Berlin after it was bombed!'* He mentions a few more places around that area that he remembers including a pub in Clase which was his local – he often drank there. He would meet his friend, his father and his uncle (who was also a scrapman) there every Friday. *'We would have a couple of jars, not too many, 10 or 12! Unfortunately, the horse didn't know the way home!'*

Ange asks him if he has any desire to reincarnate. He replies, *'If I could come back at age 45-50 I would, I really miss the female company!'* Ange asks if he could have a partner over there. He replies, *'I could if I wanted but I don't really need to.'*

Justine asks if he walks amongst us here on the earth plane. He replies, *'Yes, and I have to say, where I'm from, it's a totally different place, you call it diverse, some for the good and some for the bad, but OMG the smells coming from that kebab shop on the corner! Good God! You didn't have them in my day, see. You have to give everyone a chance, but years ago it was frowned upon.'*

Ange asks him if he has any desire to eat food over there. He says, *'We can imagine what we want to eat and drink. There's no requirement to do so but why give it up if you can think it? It's as real here as on the earth plane, even better actually.'* Gwyn is called back then and says goodbye. He had kept the vibrations high by making us laugh throughout the time he was communicating with us.

Albert returns – He says that he hopes we have enjoyed the evening. He tells us that he remembers the time when The Boy first saw a demonstration of trance in our group, saying that The Boy had nearly crawled up his cousin Mark's arm as he couldn't believe what he was seeing and hearing!

Beth asks if her mother had visited her and her two sisters last night. Albert confirms that she had indeed visited them all. Beth reveals that all three sisters had the same dream last night about their mother. Albert is delighted to hear this.

We run out of time now so Albert says goodbye.

END OF VOLUME ONE

This book is written as a journal, recounting the ongoing journey of conversations, knowledge and experiences to be shared with the world. It spans a period of just over 2 years.

Future sessions will be set out in Voloume 2.

Printed in Great Britain
by Amazon

48650730R00188